UNSOLVED

MYSTERIES OF TEXAS

UNSOLVED

MYSTERIES OF TEXAS

STORIES OF LEGENDARY OUTLAWS, BURIED TREASURE, AND HAUNTINGS IN THE LONE STAR STATE

W. C. JAMESON

TWODOT®

ESSEX, CONNECTICUT
HELENA, MONTANA

A · TWODOT® · BOOK

An imprint of Globe Pequot, the trade division of The Rowman & Littlefield Publishing Group, Inc.
4501 Forbes Blvd., Ste. 200
Lanham, MD 20706
www.rowman.com

Distributed by NATIONAL BOOK NETWORK

British Library Cataloguing-in-Publication Information available

Library of Congress Cataloging-in-Publication Data available

ISBN 978-1-4930-6148-8 (paperback: alk. paper)
ISBN 978-1-4930-6149-5 (e-book)

♾™ The paper used in this publication meets the minimum requirements of American National Standard for Information Sciences—Permanence of Paper for Printed Library Materials, ANSI/NISO Z39.48-1992.

Contents

CONTENTS

INTRODUCTION

Within the boundaries of the state of Texas can be found an impressive array of physical and cultural phenomena that exist nowhere else in America. Take environments and landscapes, for example. No other state can boast the combination of coastal regions, mountain ranges, plains, deserts, pine forests, oak-hickory forests, swamplands, brush country, and more.

And cultures. The representatives of the different cultures that make up the diversity and personality of Texas and that contributed to its success and progress over the generations include American Indians, Spanish, Mexican, French, African, German, British, Scots-Irish, Czech, Asian, and dozens of others. So great are the numbers and contributions of these various cultures that an entire building was constructed to house the examples and the history behind each. It is called the Institute of Texan Cultures and is located in San Antonio.

Texas has served as a hearth for musical styles and stylists that are known and revered around the world, including performers of blues, rock, country and western, *conjunto*, and classical. So innovative and captivating are the blend of Lone Star songwriters and performers that they have given rise to what many regard as a singular genre called Texas Music.

Texas can boast of an endless and variety-filled list of other claims, among them more than a dozen professional sports teams, dozens of colleges and universities, award-winning poets and writers, and actors.

Among the numerous features that Texas can lay claim to is that it is home to a number of baffling mysteries that have long confounded investigators, as well as the public, some for more than a century. A number of these mysteries involve outlaws. Texas has been the birthplace of noted outlaws such as John Wesley Hardin, Black Jack Ketchum, Bill Longley, and more. Others have made Texas their home or had noteworthy appearances and experiences as they were passing through. These include Sam Bass, Jesse James, Billy the Kid, John Wilkes Booth, Butch Cassidy, and others. In their wake, a number of these outlaws left behind mysteries that continue to attract the attention of researchers, investigators, and the curious. Some may be surprised at the connection between Texas and Billy the Kid, as well as John Wilkes Booth, but both of these desperados left their imprint as well as a number of lingering mysteries.

It has been said that Texas has more lost mines and buried treasures per square mile than any other state. Many of these are well documented, several have been found, but many remain elusive, continuing to lure hopeful treasure hunters, tempting them to solve the mysteries surrounding them.

Tales of hauntings around the United States are numerous, well into the tens of thousands, and most of them are simply that— tales that have been handed down over the years that have become part and parcel of the folk culture that spawned them. But in Texas, there are several recorded hauntings that have profoundly affected the citizens, hauntings that have been witnessed and experienced by hundreds yet continue to elude explanation.

And there are more. There is profound evidence of the visitation, if not settlement, of a pre-Columbian Iberian culture in Texas. That they were here is not in doubt. What became of these early explorers remains one of Texas's unsolved mysteries.

And what of the alleged UFO that crashed on the morning of April 19, 1897, in Aurora, Texas, and the alleged alien remains that were recovered? Did it really happen, or was it a hoax? The evidence is well documented, but the interpretation of such is debated and fought over today.

Spirited arguments and fistfights have erupted over interpreting the manner in which the American hero Davy Crockett met his end at the Alamo. Did he die bravely, fighting off attacking forces until the last? Or was he captured and executed, begging for his life to the end as the firing squad took aim. Or, as some claim, was Crockett taken prisoner, carried deep into Mexico, and forced to labor the remainder of his life in the silver mines?

These and other unsolved mysteries of Texas have been gathered together here. The ones selected for this book have attracted the attention of researchers for decades, and swelling bodies of evidence for each have been compiled. Absolute solutions to these mysteries, however, remain elusive. This fact only whets our appetite to learn more, to fathom the complexities associated with each, and perhaps to try to solve them. They confuse us, perplex us, and occasionally drive us mad trying to decipher them.

We love our mysteries. We crave them for any number of reasons. They challenge us, they dare us to solve them, they even taunt us in their elusiveness. They sometimes drive us to distraction. In the end, they always entertain.

OUTLAWS

CHAPTER 1

The Five Graves of Billy the Kid

History is filled with examples of individuals, both prominent and relatively unknown, who have died, were buried,
then disinterred and buried again. The reasons for such are varied:
relocation to a family cemetery, graveyard relocation as a result of
rising waters from a reservoir project, and more. Less common are
examples of individuals who have been interred three times in different locations. As unlikely as it seems, it has occurred from time
to time. A search of the historical record yielded information that
at least one individual was associated with four burial places, which
was apparently the record for such things until recently, when it
was revealed that one historical figure has been linked to *five* graves.

As improbable as it seems, the five graves are associated with
outlaw Billy the Kid, who is known to have had three graves in New
Mexico and two in Texas. Where his body currently rests, however,
is a mystery.

Billy the Kid is arguably the most famous outlaw in American history. His story has been told in hundreds of books, thousands of articles, several films, and dozens of television documentaries. In spite of the many treatments of the life of Billy the Kid, all of them virtually the same, there remain numerous mysterious and questionable elements of his life that have attracted the attention of professional researchers and investigators. They include his date and place of birth, the number of men he is credited with killing, his alleged death in 1881 at the hands of Sheriff Pat Garrett, and more. Among the mysteries is the question of where Billy the Kid is actually buried and why he is associated with five gravesites.

Hamilton, Texas, is located on the northern fringe of the Texas Hill Country, an area of rolling landscape, some open land given over to grazing, mixed forest, cedars prominent. Cattle graze throughout. Driving north on Texas State Highway 281 from the town of Hamilton, population 3,100, one encounters the Oakwood Cemetery on the east side of the road just moments before leaving the city limits. It is a county cemetery yet is maintained by the city. Near the shoulder of the road and wedged in between other headstones is a prominently displayed gravesite that proclaims "William Henry Roberts aka Billy the Kid, Born 31 December 1859, Died 27 December 1950." This odd feature likely comes as a surprise to the vast majority of Americans who long believed that the burial site for this famous outlaw was located just outside of Fort Sumner, New Mexico, on a terrace above the Pecos River and adjacent to a commercial enterprise labeled the "Billy the Kid Museum."

To further complicate matters, the aforementioned New Mexico grave and the Texas grave represent fewer than half of the burial places associated with Billy the Kid. Mysteries abound: Why so many gravesites? Who was William Henry Roberts? What is the truth?

As it turns out, much, if not most, of what the public knows about the outlaw Billy the Kid is based on material presented in an 1882 publication attributed to Sheriff Pat Garrett, the man who took credit for killing the Kid. This oft-referred to and oft-quoted book that carries the ponderous title of *The Authentic Life of Billy, the Kid: The Noted Desperado of the Southwest, Whose Deeds of Daring and Blood Have Made His Name a Terror in New Mexico, Arizona, and Northern Mexico* is filled with lies, false information, and misrepresentations. Author Frederick Nolan refers to the publication as "a farrago of nonsense" that "has been responsible for every single one of the myths perpetuated about Billy the Kid." The book, says Nolan, contains "many inaccuracies, evasions, and even untruths." Yet it is from this very book that uncountable researchers and so-called scholars have derived their information about the outlaw.

Garrett, who in truth wrote far less than half of the book if any of it at all, was a drunk, a philanderer, a debtor, an adulterer, a con man, and a politician. He was also a pathological liar. Most, if not all, of the book was written by Garrett's alcoholic friend Ashmon Upson, who was known to substitute truth for fantasy. In the end, *Authentic Life* has no credibility whatsoever, nor do any of the publications that have relied on it for source material. The life of the famous outlaw as it has been presented over the years is largely myth. The reality is somewhat different; the truth of Billy the Kid is no less exciting and compelling than the myth.

Research indicates that the body of Billy the Kid was likely never interred in at least three, and perhaps four, of the graves where he is thought to be buried. Such a mystery cum conundrum invites investigation into the reasons behind these bizarre circumstances.

The most well-known gravesite linked to Billy the Kid is located on a terrace above the floodplain of the Pecos River in the area of Fort Sumner, New Mexico. Behind the Billy the Kid Museum/Gift Shop can be found a cemetery, near the middle of which is a fenced enclosure containing a single headstone that reads "PALS" at the top, followed by the name of three individuals allegedly entombed there: Tom O'Folliard, Charlie Bowdre, and William H. Bonney, alias Billy the Kid, along with the dates of their deaths. "O'Folliard" and Bowdre were close companions of the Kid, and both were slain by law enforcement officers. "O'Folliard's" real name was Thomas O. Folliard, according to genealogical and census records. Historians simply got his name wrong. And the name "William H. Bonney" was one of several aliases assumed by the outlaw Billy the Kid.

This particular gravesite is not the one where a man, identified by Sheriff Pat Garrett as the outlaw Billy the Kid, was buried. The first burial site was in the original Fort Sumner Cemetery, and the burial was conducted under mysterious circumstances.

After Garrett shot the man he claimed was Billy the Kid, he was contradicted by one of his two deputies on the spot. The second deputy stated years later that the man slain by Garrett was not the Kid. Further, within minutes of the killing, Fort Sumner citizens were whispering about the notion that Garrett had killed the wrong man. The dead man was, they insisted, not the fugitive outlaw but a man similar in appearance. During a 1914 interview, Fort Sumner resident Arthur Hyde stated that it was not Billy the Kid who was shot by Garrett but a young Mexican who looked like him. Whatever the truth, Garrett, instead of posing for photographs with the deceased as was common practice of the day, especially for a man with a large ego, decided to have the body interred as fast as possible. This was an unusual practice, and researchers have wondered about the haste in which the burial proceeded. Could it be that Garrett did not want anyone to positively identify the body as someone other than Billy the Kid? It would seem so.

Before being transported to the cemetery, the body of the dead man was dressed in burial garb and placed in a hastily constructed wooden casket. Though difficult to verify, there is a possibility that only two or three people other than Garrett and his deputies ever saw the body of the deceased. One of them stated in print that the dead man was not Billy the Kid.

Author Leon C. Metz, in his book *Pat Garrett: The Story of a Western Lawman*, posits the possibility that passing off any body as that of Billy the Kid could easily have been done. Garrett could then petition for the reward as well as the honor and prestige that went with killing the Southwest's most noted outlaw.

Another Fort Sumner resident, John Graham, along with a Mexican helper, was sent by Garrett to the old cemetery to dig a grave shortly after the shooting. Incredibly, the cemetery was located on the floodplain of the Pecos River, a stream that was known to flood from time to time during spring rains, the rising waters extending hundreds of feet out from the banks. Most of the graves in the cemetery, twenty-six to be exact, belonged to soldiers. The grave that was later excavated for the body of the man Garrett claimed was Billy the Kid was located only a few feet from the river. Because of the controversy over whether or not Garrett actually killed the Kid, he had it dug up a year later so he could verify that it was him. Garrett was the only person who observed the remains.

In a March 1980 article that appeared in *True West* magazine, writer Ben W. Kemp, who interviewed Graham, who was his uncle, stated that Graham related that when the wagon carrying the casket of the man killed by Garrett arrived, it was accompanied by an armed guard "with strict orders to see that no one opened it to see what was inside." The word used was *what* not *who*. Four pallbearers accompanied the casket: Vicente Otero, Yginio Salazar, Jesus Silva, and Charlie Foor. The *what* becomes a bit clearer on learning that Joseph Wood, a man who assisted with the body and the casket, insisted to his dying day that the coffin contained not a man but a side of beef.

Regardless of who or what was in the casket, a wooden marker was placed at the head of the grave identifying it as that of Billy the Kid. Over the years, the marker was used as target practice by drunk soldiers, who eventually reduced it to splinters. In 1906, the remains of those buried in the original Fort Sumner cemetery were later disinterred and reburied in the Santa Fe National Cemetery. According to a 1938 interview with Carolotta Baca published in *They Knew Billy the Kid*, very few people in Fort Sumner knew the exact location of the gravesite after so many years had passed.

To complicate matters regarding the original Fort Sumner cemetery, it must be noted that during the past century and a half, the nearby Pecos River has flooded on a number of occasions. High-velocity floodwaters were observed and recorded carrying away headstones and markers, along with coffins and their contents. By the 1930s, as a result of the floodwaters, little was left of the cemetery that was recognizable. In 1937, the four pallbearers who carried the casket to the site in 1881were still alive and living in Fort Sumner. They were assembled at the old cemetery and asked to agree on the original location. They were unable to do so, each man selecting a different site. Finally, they agreed on compromise by placing a marker in the approximate center of the four different selections. This was the second "grave" of Billy the Kid. According to George E. Kaiser, there was another major flood in 1943 that washed away the newer marker.

Thus, a handful of mysteries have resulted: Where was the original location of the gravesite of the man Garrett claimed was Billy the Kid? Where was the second? And who or what was originally interred? No one knows.

Years later a "new" Billy the Kid gravesite was established by Fort Sumner officials on the first terrace above the Pecos River floodplain and a few hundred yards from the river itself. The story that accompanied this new burial place was that the Kid's body was reinterred to the new location in New Mexico. Here, a headstone was erected, a museum cum gift shop constructed nearby, and signs erected on Highway 84 to the north announcing the location of the gravesite of America's most famous outlaw to tourists. What was supposedly buried beneath the tombstone, if anything, was anybody's guess.

In 1951, the headstone was stolen. The thief was unidentified, and the marker was "lost" for twenty-six years before it was finally recovered in Granbury, Texas, and replaced at the alleged burial site in New Mexico. In February 1981, the headstone was stolen again but was recovered four days later in Huntington Beach, California. After it was returned to the Fort Sumner Cemetery, it was set in concrete. Because some visitors to the gravesite had a penchant for chipping away pieces of the headstone to take home as a souvenir, the marker was dug up, a layer of concrete poured over the graves, a new tombstone erected, and an iron fence constructed around it.

During the late 1990s, a private detective who specialized in mysteries of the Old West became interested in what might, or might not, lie beneath the newer Fort Sumner gravesite. He harbored doubts that it was the outlaw. There existed doubts among many researchers that one of the bodies was that of Billy the Kid, as advertised by the New Mexico tourist bureau and the city of Fort Sumner. The detective examined the possibility of disinterring the remains, obtaining DNA, and applying the results to his ongoing investigations of the Kid, the Lincoln County War, and more. He met with Fort Sumner mayor Raymond Lopez, explained his objectives, and promised to keep Lopez in the loop regarding his objectives. Lopez professed keen interest in the idea, and his head was filled with visions of large flocks of tourists descending on his town and spending money freely at the motels, gas stations, and cafés. The town of Fort Sumner was, and is, in large part dependent on tourism related to the notion that Billy the Kid is buried nearby.

When the detective approached Lopez again about an excavation of the gravesite, the mayor did an immediate about-face and suddenly grew hostile to the project. Did Lopez know something about the grave that he didn't want revealed? Or did he fear that if the detective found evidence that the Kid was *not* buried at this location that it might have an adverse effect on tourism?

The government of the state of New Mexico, from the office of the governor on down to city officials, has fought hard over the years to keep the myths and legends of Billy the Kid alive, including the notion that the outlaw is buried at Fort Sumner. They have, in fact, initiated a number of attempts to thwart various quests for the truth. Politics provides for an additional layer of drama and cover-up to the Billy the Kid gravesite story.

During the detective's initial phase of his investigation, then New Mexico governor Bill Richardson thought he could get some political mileage out of the activity. The governor even assigned the state medical investigator to the case. After listening to the detective lay out his theories and plans, the medical appointee, Dr. Debra Komar, traveled to Fort Sumner to examine what the state proclaimed to be the "Official Grave of Billy the Kid."

Komar excavated the gravesite. Whatever she found, the state of New Mexico wanted it covered up. She did not respond to calls or messages from the detective, refusing to communicate with him at all. The investigator suspected interference from higher levels of government, so he went into action. On January 20, 2004, Komar appeared in court in response to a subpoena.

Under oath and in response to direct questions, Komar admitted she traveled to the Fort Sumner Cemetery "on behalf of the state of New Mexico." She stated that her reception by city officials was hostile. When asked why she ceased all communications with the investigator, she responded that, on orders from above, "I was not allowed to." On the stand, Komar was asked if she believed Billy the Kid was buried at the Fort Sumner Cemetery. She replied, "I don't know. I have reason to suspect perhaps not."

What, if anything, did Komar find beneath the headstone? And why was such information withheld? The answers to those questions may have come to light seven months before her trip to Fort Sumner. The detective learned that on June 17, 2003, David Bailey, an ex-mayor of Fort Sumner, provided information that the medical investigator's office and the state of New Mexico desperately wanted kept secret. On that day, Bailey told then DeBaca County sheriff Gary Graves that he, the sheriff, needed to do something to stop the detective's investigation because "we know what's in that grave."

It was subsequently learned that, weeks earlier, Bailey and a companion had taken it upon themselves to travel to the gravesite, breach the iron fence that enclosed it, and conduct an excavation. What did they find? Nothing. There were no remains whatsoever under the headstone denoting the grave of Billy the Kid.

This tale brings us to the state of Texas. In 1948, the identity of an elderly man living in the small town of Hico, Hamilton County, Texas, was revealed by paralegal William V. Morrison to be that of the outlaw Billy the Kid. He had been going by the name of Ollie L. Roberts, one of several aliases he used throughout his life. Others included Henry McCarty, Henry Antrim, and William Bonney.

Though the old man denied the charge at first, subsequent in-depth investigation proved otherwise. His true story, as well as complete details relative to substantiating his identity, are found in *Billy the Kid: Beyond the Grave* (Jameson, 2005) and *Billy the Kid: Investigating History's Mysteries* (Jameson, 2018).

The startling findings presented in these books were attacked and criticized by some who claimed to be experts on Billy the Kid, but none came forward with even a scintilla of evidence to disprove any of them. As time passed, even more evidence was found that supported the findings. Invitations to these "experts" to participate in William Henry Roberts as Billy the Kid debates on television and in newspapers were turned down.

William Henry Roberts aka Billy the Kid passed away on December 27, 1950, from a heart episode on a Hico street while

Headstone of Ollie L. Roberts aka Billy the Kid in the Oakwood Cemetery, Hamilton, Texas

AUTHOR'S COLLECTION

walking to the post office. For much of the last couple of decades of his life, he lived on welfare. He died penniless and was buried in the paupers' section of the Oakwood Cemetery of Hamilton, twenty-one miles to the south. This was Billy the Kid's fourth grave. His headstone was a simple one. He was interred under the name he had gone by for several years—Ollie L. Roberts. It was an alias he appropriated from a cousin who died years earlier at a remote location in the West. The dead outlaw's real name, according to his own testimony and genealogical records, was William Henry Roberts.

During the 1990s, when it became clear that the evidence for Roberts being Billy the Kid was overwhelming, the town leaders of Hamilton, as with those in Fort Sumner earlier, decided to cash in on the connection. The problem was that the gravesite was in a distant portion of the Oakwood Cemetery and among a set of markers that were rarely visited. To counteract this inconvenience, the city of Hamilton decision-makers decided to make the gravesite of the famous outlaw more accessible. They placed a phony one near the shoulder of State Highway 281 within easy view of passing motorists. The City of Hamilton website touts this grave as the "real" resting place of Billy the Kid. It is the fifth grave associated with the famous outlaw.

Sometime during the first decade of the 2000s, the aforementioned detective, along with the author, traveled to the town of Hamilton, arranged for a meeting with the mayor and town council, and requested permission to disinter the remains of William Henry Roberts in order to obtain DNA samples for analysis. His request was flatly rejected with no reason given. The investigator explained to the assembled elected officials that if the DNA analysis proved once and for all that Roberts was indeed Billy the Kid, the town would benefit immensely from this connection, that people would arrive in this peaceful Texas town, stay in motels, purchase gas, and more. Despite his plea, he was turned down. During a meeting that lasted a bit more than an hour, it became clear that the city officials of Hamilton did not want the grave excavated because, as with the Billy the Kid gravesite at Fort Sumner, they knew there was nothing beneath the headstone. The Hamilton roadside gravesite, though symbolic, is a fake.

And what of the 1950 gravesite for William Henry Roberts in Hamilton? During the early 1990s, the headstone was easily located. Shortly after the book *Billy the Kid: Beyond the Grave* was released in 1995, the original grave marker disappeared, and the substitute marker next to the highway was erected. The official line of the Hamilton Chamber of Commerce and area retailers is that the recent headstone is the "real" one. When confronted with the evidence in the book, however, they confessed to the ruse.

What has become of the first headstone for Roberts aka Billy the Kid? No one admits to knowing.

Somewhere in that older part of the Hamilton cemetery lies what many consider to be the remains of the most famous outlaw in American history. In the pursuit of truth, a number of researchers and investigators continue to be eager to have access to those remains to acquire DNA.

CHAPTER 2

The Two Graves of Jesse James

If there is an American outlaw who rivals the notoriety of Billy the Kid, it's Jesse James. The two bad men had much in common: The bulk of the perceptions held by the American public of these figures were the result of dime novels, which fantasized and exaggerated their careers; each was the subject of hundreds of books and articles and dozens of films purporting to tell their stories. And both men had more than one grave.

The history books tell us that the outlaw Jesse James was shot by "the dirty little coward" (a line from the famous "The Ballad of Jesse James") Robert Ford and buried in 1882 in a cemetery on the James family farm near Kearny, Missouri, not far from the house where his mother still lived. The headstone reads:

In Loving Remembrance of My Beloved Son
Jesse James
Aged 34 Years, 6 Months, 28 Days
Murdered by a Traitor and Coward Whose
Name Is Not Worthy to Appear Here

Jesse James

Visitors come from far and wide, even from foreign countries, to gaze upon what they believe is the final resting place of the famous outlaw. In Granbury, Texas, however, can be found another headstone inscribed for the colorful bad man that reads:

Jesse Woodson James
Sept. 5, 1847 - August 15, 1951
Supposedly killed in 1882

The body of the man lying under the grass in Granbury lived much of his life going by the name J. Frank Dalton. He came to the attention of the American public in 1948, when he announced that he was, in fact, the outlaw Jesse James and that he was not killed by Robert Ford in 1882. Is there a possibility that Jesse James was not slain by Ford and went on to live much of his life in anonymity and using an alias? And who was J. Frank Dalton? Is there any possibility whatsoever that Dalton could have been Jesse James?

A brief review of the life of Jesse James is appropriate here. He was born on September 5, 1847, in Clay County, Missouri. His father, Robert James, had traveled to California to seek gold and died there in 1850. In 1852, his mother, Zerelda, with three small children, remarried. Not long afterward, however, her second husband was killed in a horse accident. In 1855, she married again, this time to Dr. Reuben Samuel, a well-respected country doctor and farmer.

When he was eighteen years of age, Jesse's older brother, Frank, enlisted in the Confederate army. He eventually joined the forces of William Clarke Quantrill, who headed a band of men who have been described as "the bloodiest guerrilla force of the Confederacy." In August 1863, Quantrill's men raided Lawrence, Kansas, a relatively defenseless town filled with noncombatants. They sacked the town and slaughtered 150 citizens.

Three months before the Lawrence raid, a contingent of Union soldiers arrived at the Samuel farm, seeking information on Quantrill's camp, which they believed to be nearby. Young Jesse was questioned but was unable to provide any information. Disappointed at Jesse's answers, the soldiers horsewhipped him and allegedly hung him by the neck for a few seconds from the rafter of a barn. Dr. Samuel was pulled from his home and also questioned. When he could provide no information, a noose was placed around his neck, and he was repeatedly hanged and cut loose from a tree in his front yard. Dr. Samuel never fully recovered from his ordeal and was eventually admitted to an asylum, where he died in 1908.

After experiencing the cruelty of the Union soldiers and watching what they did to his stepfather, Jesse developed an intense hatred of the Union, its policies, and its army. At sixteen years of age, in 1863, he joined a band of fighters led by William "Bloody Bill" Anderson. During his time with Anderson and subsequently Quantrill, Jesse James took out his hatred for the Union, killing many soldiers in the process.

At nineteen years of age, Jesse mustered out of the Confederate army. In 1874, he married and became a regular churchgoer. His hatred for Yankees did not abate, however, and he spent much of the rest of his life exacting revenge on them. He had decided to rob Yankee banks and trains.

It is somewhat unclear how many banks and trains were robbed by Jesse James and his gang. Several are documented, but a number of holdups have been attributed to him that he may not have been involved with, and it is suspected that he did perpetrate crimes that were blamed on others. As the years passed, Jesse grew weary of being pursued not only from local and state law enforcement authorities but also from the Pinkerton detectives, all of whom were finally closing in on him. There was a $10,000 reward out for Jesse James, dead or alive.

In December 1881, Jesse, his wife, and two children moved to St. Joseph, Missouri, and rented a house at 1318 Lafayette Street. He was going by the alias Thomas Howard. According to the preponderance of James-related history books, on the morning of April 3, 1882, Jesse was meeting with outlaw wannabes Bob and Charley Ford, two brothers who were cousins of Jesse. The discussion revolved around plans to rob the Platte City Bank in Kansas City, Missouri. During the discussion, Jesse noticed that a framed needlepoint made by his mother was hanging crookedly on the wall. He stepped up on a cane chair to straighten it, when Bob Ford, pulling a .38 caliber Smith & Wesson revolver, stepped up behind him and shot him in the head just below the right ear. Jesse James was dead. Or so the story goes.

Jesse's mother arrived the following day by train, and she, along with his wife, formally identified the body as that of the outlaw. The body was packed in ice and shipped by train to Kearney, where it was placed on brief display, followed by the burial in the family plot.

Less than two weeks passed following the burial of the man in Missouri identified as Jesse James, when newspapers began reporting that Robert Ford had killed a substitute, that James was still alive, and that the so-called killing was a plot to end his pursuit and eventual capture.

During the years following the alleged killing of Jesse James, more than twenty different men came forward with the claim that they were the famous outlaw. One of these claimants was a man going by the name John James. John James spent time in prison for murder, and while there, it is believed, read every available piece of literature related to the famous outlaw and decided to assume his identity. He advanced a story behind the shooting by Ford that caught the attention of researchers immediately. He claimed that the body of a Missouri outlaw named Charlie Bigelow was substituted for that of Jesse. Bigelow had conducted a handful of successful robberies and always left evidence to lead law enforcement authorities to believe that they were committed by Jesse. Bigelow did, in fact, bear a striking similarity to Jesse—same height, same general appearance. Bigelow, according to John James, was invited to Jesse's house, where he was killed and laid out on the parlor floor. The real Jesse James, he claimed, spent most of the remainder of his life in hiding.

While some lend a bit of credence to the substitution of Bigelow's body for Jesse's, the claims of John James portraying himself as the famous outlaw were never taken seriously. After being released from prison, John James went on the road, making appearances he billed as "Jesse James Alive!" He was exposed, however, by Agnes James, the widow of Frank James. She arrived at one of the performances and handed John James a pair of boots worn by Jesse and dared the performer to put them on. John James could not even come close to fitting into the size seven-and-a-half boots. John James died on December 24, 1947, in an insane asylum.

In May 1948, a man named J. Frank Dalton appeared on the scene. From his home in Lawton, Oklahoma, Dalton, who was not related to any of the gang members of the same name, announced he was the real Jesse James and claimed to be 101 years old. Within days, a number of Jesse James aficionados, as well as old acquaintances of the outlaw, jumped onto the Dalton bandwagon and supported his contention, lending a level of credence and support for the claim. Dalton was represented by a man named Orvus Lee Howk, who made it known that Dalton was available for personal appearances and would sign autographs. Howk's presence immediately invited suspicion to the Dalton claim—Howk stated that *his* real name was Jesse Lee James III, that he was the grandson of the notorious Jesse James, and that Dalton was, indeed, his grandfather. It must be pointed out here that no documentation has ever surfaced to prove Howk's claim.

Dalton's claim generated a significant number of headlines in newspapers across the nation, including three lengthy reports by famed author Robert Ruark in the New York *World Telegram.* Ruark was convinced of the accuracy of Dalton's claims. Dalton also repeated the previous claim by John James that the body of outlaw Charlie Bigelow had been substituted for Jesse's and stated that Bigelow "looked enough like me to be my own twin."

A handful of Jesse James researchers have attempted to make the case that the substitution of Bigelow for the outlaw was part of a plot engineered by Jesse and former members of Quantrill's Raiders and that the Ford brothers were part of the conspiracy. They are also convinced that Jesse's wife and mother were in on the scheme. It was learned that, on her initial viewing of the body

J. Frank Dalton aka Jesse James

of the dead man, Jesse's mother said, "That is not my son." She was taken aside by one of the confederates, who explained to her that the shooting had been staged and that it was for Jesse's protection. She subsequently returned to view the body a second time and told those assembled that it was her son.

A writer for the popular magazine of the day, *Police Gazette*, interviewed Dalton in 1948. He claimed that Dalton possessed all of the scars reportedly borne by Jesse, including rope burns around his neck from when he was supposedly hung by Union soldiers.

Another writer by the name of Rudy Turilli appointed himself pro-moter of Dalton and secured him appearances on television. Turilli self-published a dreadful pamphlet, the sole purpose of which was to promote the old man as Jesse James. It was apparently never fact-checked and was replete with errors and misrepresentations. Turilli offered a $10,000 reward to anyone who could prove that Dalton was not Jesse James. Stella James, a relative, along with two of Jesse's grandchildren met the challenge and hauled Turilli into circuit court in Franklin, Missouri, in 1970. The judge instructed Turilli to pay the family the $10,000. Turilli passed away not long afterward. Not a cent of the money was ever paid.

Homer Croy, author of *Jesse James Was My Neighbor*, inter-viewed Dalton after the book was published, asking him basic questions about Jesse and his family. Dalton, it was reported, "failed miserably."

The aged and somewhat ailing J. Frank Dalton was once pho-tographed in a bed surrounded by a cadre of his so-called outlaw friends, at least two authentic but the rest imposters. One of the real outlaws was Al Jennings, a former train robber. Jennings went on record as stating that Dalton was Jesse James. Years later, Jennings, when asked why he went along with the notion that Dalton was Jesse James, replied, "Why not? They paid me a hundred dollars!"

During the short time that J. Frank Dalton was alive follow-ing his claim to be Jesse James, a small group of believers rushed to lend support. They brought with them "proof" that what the old man was saying was true. It was said by the Dalton supporters that he bore all of the same scars and evidence of bullet wounds as Jesse.

The opposition insisted he did not. None of the so-called proof ever held up under investigation.

Dalton's inability to respond correctly to some Jesse James–related questions, his supporters insisted, was due to his advanced years and that he could not be expected to remember everything. If anything, the excitement surrounding the notion that Dalton could be the famous outlaw grew and spread throughout the 1950s and 1960s. Three of Jesse James's grandsons—Jesse Quanah James, Burleigh Dale James, and Charles A. James—went on record as stating that J. Frank Dalton was their grandfather.

At this writing, a DNA test is being planned by a Dalton-as-James supporter to prove the old man's claim once and for all. What is not clear, however, is the source of the DNA sample or samples.

Those in opposition to Dalton's claim insisted he was a charlatan and only one of many Jesse James imposters. (There were twenty-six in all at last count.) Others insisted that Dalton was able to provide specific details about incidents involving the outlaw as well as personal encounters with James's associates. Dalton was never taken seriously by professional historians, however.

Investigation has also revealed that Jesse James was not the first famous identity claimed by Dalton. During the 1930s and 1940s, Dalton made the claim that he was the noted Western lawman John Franklin Dalton. When it was eventually proven in 1948 that the real J. F. Dalton, a US Marshal for the Oklahoma Territory, died in the line of duty in 1887, this Dalton lost little time in switching his identity to that of Jesse James. This, of course, created an immense credibility gap.

To further jeopardize J. Frank Dalton's trustworthiness, he surrounded himself with promoters who possessed reputations as scam artists with little regard for the truth, men such as Houck and Turilli. Today, the most vocal supporters of J. Frank Dalton as Jesse James lack credibility among the community of qualified professional historians and writers. On the other hand, the credentialed historians have been proven in error time and again in recent years, particularly in the case of Billy the Kid.

If J. Frank Dalton was not Jesse James, and most of the pertinent evidence points in the direction that he wasn't, then who was he? Most who have examined the life and times of Dalton are certain that the very name was an alias, and no one is clear as to his true identity. There exists some evidence, though no proof, that Dalton may have been involved in one or more bank and/or train robberies as a young man and that he did so using the name Jesse James, leading some to speculate that there were two men involved in such activity, both of them going by the name Jesse James. The mystery deepens.

J. Frank Dalton, the man who claimed to be the outlaw Jesse James, passed away in Granbury, Texas, on August 15, 1951, but the controversy did not die with him. To put the matter to rest, theoretically, a man named James E. Starrs, a professor of law and forensic science at Georgetown University, received a grant from said institution, as well as permission from the James family, to exhume the body buried in the James family plot in Kearny, Missouri, in order to conduct a DNA examination. Starrs, along with a team of fifteen men of science, undertook to exhume the remains in July 1995.

From the grave, the excavators retrieved more than twenty skull fragments, leg bones, collarbones, and fragments of other bones, along with fourteen teeth. The bones were shipped to a crime lab in Kansas then to Kansas State University for cleaning, X-raying, and cataloging. Bone samples to be used for DNA testing were sent to Pennsylvania State University and to Cellmark Laboratories in Maryland. On February 26, 1996, Starrs presented his findings to the convention of the Academy of Forensic Sciences in Nashville, Tennessee. In summary, Starrs stated the mitochondrial DNA in the bones and two of the teeth from the grave compared to blood samples from two descendants of Jesse James and that there was a "better than ninety-nine percent certainty" that the bones in the grave belonged to Jesse James.

For many, the Starrs investigation closed the case on Jesse James and his imposters forever. Others were not so sure. The notion was advanced that the bones and teeth from the grave were too degraded by groundwater to yield a legitimate DNA result. In an interesting twist, Starrs's reputation was attacked, with critics claiming that he was more interested in publicity than in legitimate scientific findings, a claim echoed by several, including his own colleagues.

To lend further assault and insult to Starrs's investigation was the charge that the DNA test was made on a tooth that did *not* come from the grave at all but from a desk drawer in the Jesse James Museum. The provenance of the tooth has never been verified.

Further, Starrs's investigative findings do *not* necessarily point to the notion that there is a "ninety-nine percent certainty" that the remains found in the grave belonged to Jesse James. What it does point to is that the remains could, based on the DNA test, belong to someone *related* to Jesse James. Investigation has revealed that Charlie Bigelow, whose body was allegedly substituted for that of Jesse's, was a relative of the James family.

So, who in the heck was J. Frank Dalton? His life, as was the life (and death) of the real Jesse James, is fraught with mysteries that researchers are still trying to unravel. Is there a possibility, however remote, that Dalton could have been Jesse James? His ardent supporters believe so.

CHAPTER 3

Did Outlaw Bill Longley Escape the Gallows?

Texas outlaw Bill Longley never garnered the notoriety and newspaper headlines as did other western bad men. Nor did Longley inspire the dime novelists to any degree to recreate and fantasize his adventures and outlawry for readers as they did with Billy the Kid, Jesse James, and others. In spite of the comparative paucity of publicity generated by this hardened killer, fact and lore long associated with his exploits combine to suggest he may have killed well over thirty men.

William Preston Longley was born on October 6, 1851, near Mills Creek in Austin County, Texas, the sixth of ten children. At sixteen years of age, Longley quit school and began running around with a gang of toughs, drinking, and engaging in lawless behavior. At an early age, he had demonstrated skill with guns and a propensity for violence. At least one account states that when he was fifteen years old, Longley killed his first man, a deed that allegedly troubled him not at all and one that he never regretted.

According to the tale, the year was 1866, and Central Texas, as well as other parts of the South, was recovering from the aftermath of the Civil War and suffering the ongoing processes related to the establishment of Union rule. Austin County, like many other locations in Texas, was filling up with carpetbaggers, Union officials, and Yankee politicians and businessmen, a trend that antagonized the local residents.

With the end of the Civil War, a brand new Texas state police force was created and consisted, in part, of a number of newly freed slaves. Most of them carried out their jobs honorably. A few, imbued with a newfound sense of power, often went out of their way to aggravate Texas's white settlers.

One afternoon, according to an oft-told tale, a young Bill Longley was walking down the main street of the tiny community of Old Evergreen, located eight miles northeast of Giddings in Lee County. (Over time, Old Evergreen, bypassed by major railroads, was abandoned. Today, it is part of the town of Lincoln.). Longley paused to watch a newly arrived black policeman riding through town. As the policeman guided his mount along the narrow road, he loudly cursed the whites who were watching him from the stores and staring from the sidewalks. From time to time, the lawman raised his rifle and pointed it at one of the townsfolk. One of the white men who received a loud cursing and found himself looking down the barrel of the policeman's rifle was Bill Longley's father.

Confidently, the younger Longley stepped out into the middle of the street, faced the policeman, and told him to put his gun away. Stunned that this youthful intruder would challenge him, the lawman merely stared dumbfounded at the boy. It was his undoing.

In a flash, Longley pulled out a pistol and shot the officer out of his saddle, killing him instantly.

Given the strong anti-Union sentiments at the time, townspeople carried the body of the dead policeman away and buried him in an unmarked grave. Young Longley, rather than being charged with the killing, was thereafter regarded as a hero in the town.

This experience, according to some writers, shaped the violent personality of Bill Longley and initiated a spate of ruthless killings that extended over the next several years. There is, however, one problem with the account: In spite of the oft-repeated story of Longley killing the policeman, not a single shred of evidence exists to verify that the incident ever occurred. Evidence does exist, however, that Longley was indeed involved in other killings.

The year was 1868, and Bill Longley was seventeen years of age. In December of that year, three former slaves—Green Evans, Pryer Evans, and a man known only as Ned—were riding through Old Evergreen when they were approached by Longley in the company of two friends. Longley and his partners pointed revolvers at the riders and forced them into a dry creek bed, where they intended to rob them. Realizing what was about to happen, Green Evans spurred his horse, but as he rode away, Longley fired several shots in his direction, the bullets knocking Evans from his horse. He died moments later. Longley and his friends ran to the dead man and removed items from his pockets while Pryer Evans and Ned escaped.

Longley eventually decided to leave the area. Making a decent living in Central Texas during post–Civil War days was difficult for most, but it was especially so for a young man like Longley. He longed for something better than sharecropping or serving as a blacksmith's apprentice. This disenchantment for life in Old Evergreen, accompanied by his growing spirit of adventure, took hold of Bill Longley. One day he rode away to seek his fortune elsewhere.

Life was not much better in other places, at least not at first. During the next several months, Longley drifted from one cow camp to another, from one corn farm to the next. His travels took him to Arkansas, Oklahoma, Kansas, Wyoming, and the Dakotas. The young man soon tired of ranch and farm work and cast about for other ways of making a living. He became attracted to gambling and in a short time grew adept at cards. At one time he operated a saloon in the Black Hills of South Dakota, where he successfully separated newfound gold from the miners at the bar and the gaming tables.

During this time, Bill Longley committed a number of robberies and holdups, and it is certain that he killed several men in the process. Longley was earning a reputation as a man with a fierce temper, and some claimed that he killed during fits of anger. Others have written that he killed for the sheer joy of watching men die. According to some researchers, several of Longley's murders took place from ambush. In other cases, his victims were goaded into fights by the confident and quick-drawing gunman.

On at least one occasion, Longley killed out of paranoia. Once, while working as a cowhand, Longley shot and killed a man who was merely looking at him. He said he couldn't sleep because the cowboy just sat and watched him all the time. One night Longley became so aggravated at being watched that he crawled out of his bedroll, picked up a gun, and shot the man in the head. After holstering his weapon, Longley climbed back into his bedroll and fell asleep immediately.

In June 1870, Longley enlisted in the US Army and was assigned to a cavalry regiment. He deserted two weeks later, was

Bill Longley

captured, court-martialed, and sentenced to two years in a military prison. For reasons unexplained, he was released four months later and shipped back to his cavalry unit. He deserted again in May 1872.

Longley returned to Texas in February 1873. During the next three years, the volatile and ill-tempered Longley killed several more men, was arrested a number of times, and either managed to escape or was released. Longley, who eventually became known as Wild Bill Longley and Bloody Bill Longley, has been described by some writers as a serial killer, a description that appears to be accurate. Tiring of the constant pursuit and harassment by lawmen in Texas, Longley fled to Louisiana.

On June 6, 1877, Longley, while residing in De Soto Parish and going by the alias Bill Jackson, was arrested by Nacogdoches County (Texas) sheriff Milt Mast for the murder of Wilson Anderson. Anderson, a childhood friend of Longley, was shot at the instigation of Caleb Longley, Bill's uncle. Caleb blamed Anderson for the death of his son and talked Bill Longley into taking revenge. Bill Longley was arrested and transported back to Giddings, Texas, where he was tried, convicted, and sentenced to hang. On October 11, 1878, area newspapers carried the report that Bill Longley was executed in Giddings, Texas, only a few miles from his birthplace near Old Evergreen.

Whether or not it was Bill Longley who was hanged, however, was controversial at the time and remains a mystery to this day. A handful of researchers are convinced the killer never met his fate on the gallows but was allowed to escape. Some evidence suggests that he returned to Louisiana, where he lived out the remainder of his life using the alias of John Calhoun Brown.

The facts surrounding the hanging are confusing and dramatically conflicting. At least one account claims Longley was executed in front of "a crowd of 4,000." Another account states that Longley was escorted out of town by the sheriff and a deputy and allegedly hung with only the two lawmen present. Still others claim another prisoner, a Longley look-alike and a presumed relative, was hung in the killer's place. The body of the hanged man was subjected to a hasty burial the same day in the Giddings cemetery. A marker, a piece of petrified wood, was erected over the site.

A short time after the alleged hanging, a story made the rounds of Lee, Burleson, Travis, and Austin Counties that the sheriff who was given the responsibility of carrying out the hanging was bribed by Longley and that the lawman helped the gunman escape to Louisiana. Another version of the alleged execution, this one from the outlaw's kin in Giddings, suggested that Longley and the sheriff were friends and that the lawman aided the outlaw's escape out of loyalty. Bill Longley's father, Campbell, came forward several years after the hanging and claimed that his son's death had been faked.

As time passed, more curious tales about Bill Longley surfaced. One of the most intriguing concerned a Louisiana farmer and businessman who went by the name of John Calhoun Brown. Brown was a somewhat reclusive and mysterious figure and very little is known about him. According to the accounts, Brown showed up in a small Louisiana community two weeks after Bill Longley was presumably hanged. He purchased a farm and during the ensuing years made a good living growing cotton. A few Central Texas residents who knew Longley and encountered Brown in Louisiana maintained they were the same man. It was also related that members of the Longley family always knew the killer escaped the gallows to live out the remainder of his life in Louisiana. According to historical documents, John Calhoun Brown, aka Bill Longley, died in 1926.

Over the years, a number of Bill Longley researchers began to wonder who was actually buried in the Giddings cemetery— Longley or a substitute. As time passed, the marker identifying the so-called Longley gravesite was accidentally removed, and for years no one was certain of its exact location.

One of the people interested in whether or not it was Bill Longley who was buried at Giddings was anthropologist Douglas Owsley. Owsley, associated with the Smithsonian Institution, was sent to Giddings to try to find some answers.

During the summer of 1998, Owsley, accompanied by his assistants and using a 1920 photograph of the gravesite, identified what they believed to be the location where the hanged man was buried. After receiving permission from authorities, the scientists dug into the site and found several teeth and some bones. Owsley stated that the bones belonged to "a tall man who died young." The remains were sent to the University of Texas at San Antonio for study and then forwarded to the Smithsonian for further analysis.

It was officially reported in June 2001 that "the remains from the grave site were indeed those of Bill Longley." Some concern exists that Owsley, a highly credentialed anthropologist, overstated the result of his findings. Based on the DNA testing, the enduring fact is that the remains disinterred from the questionable grave site belonged to someone who was *related* to the descendants of the Longley family. A conclusion was thus formed that the bones were those of outlaw Bill Longley when, in fact, they could have belonged to a relative.

The conclusion that the remains belonged to the outlaw Bill Longley, according to some, may have been premature as well as suspect. Several longtime Giddings residents, along with a number of Longley relatives, have claimed that the grave that was excavated was *not* the location where Bill Longley was supposed to have been buried. Other relatives maintain that the bones that were disinterred and tested for DNA belonged not to Bill Longley but to a close relative who had been buried there. Since a number of Longley's kin have been buried in the Giddings cemetery, this remains a distinct possibility.

These days, according to a Longley relative who was interviewed for this book, several members of the family are satisfied that the outlaw was indeed hanged in Giddings and that his remains rest in the cemetery. Other Longley descendants, however, are not convinced and don't hesitate to quote family lore that holds to the belief that their infamous ancestor did, in fact, escape the gallows and flee to Louisiana to live out the remainder of his life using the alias John Calhoun Brown.

CHAPTER 4

The Mystery of the Bowie Bank Robbery Loot

Outlaws come in all shapes and sizes, races, religions, and genders. Some have become more famous than others. A survey taken during the 1990s asked people to name US presidents who served during the latter half of the nineteenth century. Hardly any of the respondents could name one. On the other hand, when asked to name American outlaws who robbed and killed during that same time period, they were able to cite Billy the Kid, Jesse James, Butch Cassidy, the Doolin Gang, the Dalton Gang, and others. Though Billy the Kid et al. are well known as a result of books, articles, and film, the truth is most outlaws went about their business flying under the radar, so to speak, and the names of most of them are all but unknown to the majority of the American public. Such is the case with the four men who robbed a bank in the town of Bowie, Montague County, Texas, in 1894. A greater mystery, however, relates to what became of the twenty-dollar gold pieces and other currency they stole. It is known that the coins were buried, but what became of this cache has perplexed law enforcement authorities as well as treasure hunters for well over a century. The hoard of gold coins, worth millions, is still searched for today.

Early one morning in late spring 1894, four strangers rode into Bowie, Texas, a growing agricultural community located fifteen miles south of the Oklahoma border and sixty-two miles northwest of Fort Worth. With studied casualness, the men lingered for a time near the town's only bank until the manager arrived to unlock the doors. After exchanging greetings, the four men followed the manager into the building, giving him the impression that they wished to conduct business.

Once inside the bank, the strangers pulled their revolvers and ordered the manager to fill several canvas sacks with gold coins and paper money. Before he had completed the task, two bank employees arrived for work and surprised the robbers. One of the bandits panicked and began firing his weapon at the newcomers, wounding one. Grabbing the few bags that had been filled with coins and cash, the robbers ran from the bank to their horses, which had been tethered at a hitch rail. After tying the sacks of loot onto their saddles, the outlaws mounted up and fled from the town.

During the getaway, the bandits exchanged gunfire with several citizens who had raced to the scene. One resident was killed in the crossfire, and the robbers escaped unharmed. Within the hour, a posse was organized and left in pursuit of the outlaws.

The bank manager later reported that the bandits absconded with a total of ten thousand dollars in twenty-dollar gold pieces, along with eighteen thousand dollars in assorted coins and currency.

The robbers rode north toward Rock Crossing, an important ford on the Red River. If they managed to cross the river, they would be relatively safe in the lawless environs of Indian Territory (today Oklahoma). The Territory, as it was called then, was perceived as a safe haven by criminals because of the paucity of law enforcement found there. Only weeks earlier, however, a small detachment of federal marshals had been assigned to the region just north of the Red River by Judge Isaac Parker, the famous "hanging judge" of Fort Smith, Arkansas, and given the responsibility of enforcing the law in the Territory.

On arriving at Rock Crossing, the bank robbers received an unwelcome surprise. As a result of recent heavy spring rains, the Red River was well above flood stage and impossible to cross. Unaware of any pursuit, the outlaws decided to make camp in a grove of cottonwood trees on the south bank of the river and attempt to cross in the morning, when they believed the water level would be lower and safer. That evening, the men split the paper money from the robbery but left the gold coins tied up in the canvas sacks. In the meantime, the posse was doggedly following the trail of the outlaws in spite of the rain.

When the Bowie city marshal realized that the bank robbers were headed north, he notified the federal marshals he knew to be stationed across the river in Indian Territory. Since Rock Crossing was the only safe place to ford the Red River for several miles in either direction, the marshals headed in that direction in hopes of encountering them.

When the outlaws awoke at daybreak the following day, they noted that the level of the river had dropped significantly.

Following a quick breakfast, they saddled their mounts and loaded their gear. They were preparing to cross the river when one of them spotted the posse approaching the campsite from a half mile away. Fearing that the weight of the sacks of gold coins might jeopardize their escape across the river, they hurriedly scooped out a shallow hole by a large cottonwood tree, deposited the loot in the excavation, and covered it.

With the posse close enough to shoot at them, the four outlaws hurriedly mounted their horses and raced toward the river. Plunging into the swiftly moving stream, they made for the opposite bank. Though the water level was lower than the previous day, the crossing proved difficult and dangerous. On several occasions, horses and men went under and resurfaced farther downstream. Finally, the exhausted and frightened outlaws and horses made their way to the other side. After climbing the low bank and heading to a nearby grove of trees, they were surprised by the federal marshals, who had arrived only moments earlier. Offering no resistance whatsoever, the four bank robbers meekly surrendered to the lawmen.

Most of the paper money and a few of the coins were recovered from the outlaws' saddlebags, but none of the twenty-dollar gold pieces or the majority of the other coins were to be found. On questioning, the four bandits denied any knowledge of the gold coins.

One of the marshals, a man named Palmore, was given the responsibility of delivering the bank robbers to Fort Smith, where they were to stand trial for the robbery of the First National Bank of Bowie, Texas, along with the murder of one citizen. Palmore, accompanied by one additional marshal, escorted the robbers on the long journey to Fort Smith and the awaiting hanging judge. Along the way, Palmore and the oldest of the robbers engaged in friendly conversation and often played cards together by the campfire in the evenings. On several occasions, Palmore questioned the outlaw about the twenty-dollar gold pieces known to have been taken from the bank, but the bandit would merely smile and wink at the lawman.

Weeks later, the four bank robbers appeared in the courtroom of Judge Parker. The trial was quick and judgment swift: All four men were found guilty of bank robbery and murder and were sentenced to hang.

On the day set for the execution, Palmore, along with several other deputies, was ordered to escort the outlaws to the gallows located just outside the courthouse. The four were noticeably pale, both from spending several weeks in the dark chamber of the jail cell located beneath the courthouse, as well as from fear and apprehension of dying on the gallows. Palmore assisted each of the manacled bank robbers up the thirteen steps to the gallows platform. The last outlaw in line, Palmore's card-playing associate, turned to him and winked once again.

The hangman placed a black hood over the head of each of the condemned men before securing a noose around his neck. As the second prisoner was pushed forward to receive his hood, the fourth outlaw leaned toward Palmore once more and whispered that the gold coins were buried beneath a large tree near where the outlaws were camped the night before they were caught. Again, the bank robber winked at Palmore and then stepped forward to meet his fate after being hooded and roped.

Several months passed before Palmore could find an opportunity to return to the area of the outlaws' last campsite. Because he had never crossed the river and inspected the Texas side on the day of the capture, Palmore never actually saw the outlaws' camp and was unsure of its exact location. The area was a well-used ford and stopping place, and there were several campsites in the timber along the high bank on the Texas side of the stream.

Palmore believed the outlaw's story and was convinced the cache of gold coins could be found. Selecting a likely campsite, Palmore dug around the bases of several large trees. Finding nothing, he moved to another campsite and made more excavations. His searches proved unsuccessful.

Because of his obligations as a federal marshal, Palmore couldn't remain in the area for long. He returned on other occasions and conducted more excavations, but success continued to elude him.

A handful of researchers who have devoted some time to this episode are convinced that the cache of twenty-dollar gold pieces is located close to the confluence of the Red River and the Little Wichita River in a grove of cottonwoods. In recent years, however, some of the woods in this region have been cleared to extend cropland. It is possible, according to some, that the cache may lie a few inches below the surface of a cotton field.

Others have suggested that the twenty-dollar gold pieces were buried close to the riverbank. Still others argue that if the Red River had been in flood stage, the water likely would have covered the bank and thus any campsite located there. Assuming the coins were somehow buried close to the riverbank, erosion by the Red River during the ensuing years may have uncovered the cache and washed it to the bottom of the stream. Most, however, are convinced that the cache lies well back from the riverbank and thus safe from the ravages of floodwaters.

Whatever the case, there is no evidence that the twenty-dollar gold pieces taken in the Bowie bank robbery have ever been found. Today it has been estimated that the outlaws' cache would be worth nearly sixteen times its original value, and whoever finds it would become wealthy. The mystery of its location remains.

CHAPTER 5

John Wilkes Booth in Texas

During the early 1860s, John Wilkes Booth was the most celebrated, most popular actor in the Washington, DC, area if not along the entire eastern seaboard from Virginia to New York. His performances in Shakespeare's *Hamlet* and *Richard III* endeared him to theatergoers and generated headlines in area newspapers. Booth, however, is most famous for his role in the assassination of President Abraham Lincoln.

Contrary to what most history books state, compelling evidence accumulated since the 1960s has yielded insight into the notion that the assassin was not killed by soldiers in 1865 in Virginia, as previously reported, but rather escaped to live another thirty-eight years. (See *John Wilkes Booth: Beyond the Grave*, Jameson, 2013.)

After fleeing the nation's capital following the assassination, Booth eventually left the country, only to return years later. Traveling incognito, he reportedly resided for a time in Tennessee, Louisiana, and elsewhere under a variety of aliases. Eventually, Booth

John Wilkes Booth

moved to Texas, where he resided for twenty years. There, his true identity was learned.

History records that on the evening of April 14, 1865, President Abraham Lincoln was assassinated by the renowned actor John Wilkes Booth at Ford's Theater in Washington, DC. After shooting Lincoln in the back of the head, Booth leapt from the presidential box to the stage and shouted, "*Sic semper tyrannis!*" ("Thus always to tyrants!")

His murderous act accomplished, Booth ran across the stage and out of the theater into a dark alley to a horse that was being tended by an unsuspecting theater employee. After leaping into the saddle, Booth guided the horse out of the alley and raced eastward toward the Anacostia River. Moments later, he crossed the bridge into Maryland. Days later, according to authorities, a man resembling Booth had made his way into Virginia and was taking refuge at the farm of Richard Garrett near the town of Port Royal.

The commanders of the military pursuit learned of this and headed to the farm. On arriving at the location, the military discovered their quarry was hiding in the tobacco barn. One of the leaders of the pursuit, Lieutenant Lafayette Baker, attempted to convince the man to surrender. When he refused, the order was given to set fire to the barn in the hope of driving the hunted man into the open. As the flames crawled up one side of the structure and smoke began filling the interior, an enlisted man, Thomas P. Corbett, despite orders to the contrary, made his way to one side of the barn, peering through the wide spaces between the structure's planks, and spotted the fugitive inside. Corbett took aim at the fugitive and fired his pistol. The bullet entered the right side of the man's head below the ear, penetrated the vertebrae, and exited on the left side.

The seriously wounded victim dropped to the ground. Soldiers rushed in and moments later pulled him from the burning structure. Badly wounded, the man was carried to the front porch of the Garrett house and placed on a mattress. There, he moaned in pain for hours, finally expiring at 7 a.m. Within minutes of the death of the man the US government claimed was John Wilkes

Booth, the assassin of President Abraham Lincoln, subdued conversation began to filter through the throng of soldiers and others at the scene that the dead man was *not* Booth. Booth had dark brown hair and a brown mustache but no beard. The dead man on the mattress had red hair and a substantial red beard. Farmer Garrett told the authorities that the visitor had identified himself as James W. Boyd and had asked to spend the night.

Curiously, the body of the man identified as Booth was about to undergo a strange journey. Via an extremely roundabout route, it was eventually transported back to the Washington Navy Yard and placed aboard a vessel. A number of individuals were permitted to view the body. Some of them identified it as that of Booth, but it was learned later that those who did barely knew the man. Others claimed it was not the actor. It is difficult to understand, but none of the Booth family members or close friends of the assassin were allowed to view the remains. The government summoned photographer Alexander Gardner to capture an image of the dead man. Garner was supervised and directed by War Department detective James A. Wardell. Gardner was allowed to take only a single photograph. When developed, it, along with the plate, was immediately seized. Later, the government denied that any photographs were ever taken of the body. To this day, no one knows the whereabouts of the photograph.

What eventually became of the body of the man the government claimed was John Wilkes Booth has given rise to additional mysteries. One account states that it was secretly interred in the floor of the Washington, DC, Arsenal. Another tale has the body carried out to sea and thrown overboard. But then on February 15, 1869, the remains of the man the US government insisted was John Wilkes Booth was turned over to the Booth family in Baltimore. It was delivered to the undertaking establishment of Harvey and Marr in Baltimore. The remains, which by this time consisted of little more than a skeleton with only bits of flesh and hair remaining, was viewed by dozens of Booth family members and friends. One of the viewers was Basil Moxley, a longtime friend of Booth. Moxley noted that the skeleton had red hair and said it was "not Booth but rather another man." Others who viewed the remains expressed doubt that they belonged to John Wilkes Booth. The skeleton was later buried in the Booth family plot.

If the man shot and killed at Garrett's barn was not Booth, as more and more investigators have come to believe, then what happened to the assassin? Curiously, while a contingent of the US military tracked a suspect to Garrett's barn, saw him killed, and declared him to be Booth, a separate group of soldiers followed the trail of another suspect westward. Along the way, the evidence accumulated that the soldiers were on the trail of the real Booth but were never able to catch up to him. The evidence led the pursuers to believe that Booth, during the ensuing weeks, made his way to Canada and thence to England, where he remained for a few years. Booth subsequently traveled to India, where he joined an acting troupe, performing roles in his favorite plays, *Richard III* and *Hamlet*. He was listed in theater programs as "John Booth Wilkes." There is also evidence that Booth's sister in Baltimore received several letters from him while he was in India. Some researchers suggest that Booth died in India, but documentation is lacking. There does exist, however, compelling evidence that the man believed by many to be the most famous assassin in history returned to the United States and resided and earned his living in Texas.

Despite the official government position that John Wilkes Booth was shot and killed and that the case of the assassination was closed, rumors abounded that he was still alive. The assassin was also allegedly spotted in Ceylon on several occasions. Andrew Jackson Donelson, once a close companion of Booth, claimed to have encountered the assassin on a Pacific Island in the late 1860s. According to Donelson, Booth asked him not to tell anyone. At one point during their conversation, Booth handed Donelson a gold medallion and asked him to deliver it to his brother, Edwin Booth.

Ex-soldier, lawyer, and statesman General Albert Pike resided in Washington, DC. One of his favorite actors was John Wilkes Booth, and Pike attended his plays on several occasions. One evening while drinking with old friend Colonel M. W. Connally in the Pickwick Hotel in Fort Worth, Texas, Pike's gaze wandered to the mirror behind the bar. There, he saw the image of a man he recognized immediately. Turning, he stared directly at the customer seated a few tables away and exclaimed, "My God! It's John Wilkes Booth!" With that, the man at the table jumped up and ran out of the bar. Over the years since his alleged killing, Booth had been seen by friends and others on numerous occasions.

During the 1870s, a man going by the name of John St. Helen was living and operating a saloon in Glen Rose, Texas, fifty-four miles southwest of Fort Worth. One day, St. Helen visited a lawyer named Finis L. Bates, who had an office in Granbury, seventeen miles away, and asked him to defend him against a charge of running a saloon without a license. St. Helen admitted to Bates that he was, indeed, guilty of the charge but stated that he would resist appearing at a court hearing. The barkeeper told Bates that his real name was not John St. Helen and that he was concerned that his true identity might be discovered. The risk, he said, was too great.

Several weeks later, St. Helen moved to Granbury, and he and Bates became close friends. According to Bates's notes, St. Helen bore a remarkable resemblance to John Wilkes Booth and showed an "intimacy with every detail of theater work." St. Helen subscribed to several theater-related periodicals, could recite most of Shakespeare's plays, and was particularly fond of *Richard III*.

Late one night, Bates was summoned to St. Helen's bedside. St. Helen told Bates he was seriously ill and did not think he would live. He told Bates to search under his pillow, where he would find a tintype. Bates retrieved an image of John St. Helen. St. Helen asked Bates to send the tintype to Edwin Booth in Baltimore with a note stating that the man in the picture had passed away. St. Helen then placed a hand on Bates's arm and confessed that he was, in fact, John Wilkes Booth, the assassin of President Abraham Lincoln. The stunned Bates promised that he would do as requested and sat up with St. Helen through the night.

St. Helen remained seriously ill for several weeks, eventually began improving, and in time recovered. When he was able, he invited Bates to walk with him along a tree-lined path a short distance out of Granbury. During the walk, St. Helen once again told the lawyer that he was Booth, and he pleaded with Bates to keep the knowledge secret. He went on to provide significant details relative to his life as Booth, the assassination of President Lincoln, and his escape.

Bates wrote in his book *The Escape and Suicide of John Wilkes Booth* that St. Helen told him that the principal instigator of the slaying of Lincoln was the vice president, Andrew Johnson. St. Helen claimed that he, Booth, visited with Johnson on the afternoon of April 14, 1865, only four hours before the assassination and that the vice president informed him that it had been arranged for General Ulysses Grant to be out of town and that the way had been cleared to facilitate the escape from Ford's Theater into Maryland without interference from the military.

Initially, Bates was disbelieving that President Lincoln's assassination was the culmination of a conspiracy. Throughout the conversation, however, St. Helen related a number of precise details relative to the murder of Lincoln, the subsequent escape from Ford's Theater, and the flight through the Maryland and Virginia countryside; details that differed markedly from the accounts provided by the US government. Researchers who have examined Bates's account maintain that the information could have come from only someone with intimate experience regarding these events. The specifics provided by St. Helen were unknown to historians at the time. If St. Helen were merely an imposter, one must wonder why he did not relate commonly accepted and widely publicized aspects of the assassination and escape but instead told of an entirely different and quite probable account that conflicted with the government version of events.

One particularly telling piece of information concerns Booth's diary. The official version relates that it was taken from the pockets of the dying man at Garrett's farm. According to journals and papers analyzed by a handful of researchers, however, Booth's diary was lost in a grove of trees at a location near Gambo Creek, where he had camped at one point during his escape. St. Helen told Bates that, on April 22, he discovered that he had lost his diary, some letters, and a photograph of his sister. The information that Booth's diary and other items were actually found at Gambo Creek did not come to light until one hundred years later. There is no possible way that St. Helen could have learned such a thing from another source.

St. Helen told Bates he decided to come to Texas after spending a year in New Orleans, where he taught school and went by the alias Ney. When he arrived in Glen Rose, he adopted the name John St. Helen and opened a saloon. He moved to Granbury in 1872.

St. Helen aka John Wilkes Booth remained in Texas for at least the next twenty years, mostly in and around Granbury. Other than Finis Bates, he never told anyone else he was John Wilkes Booth during this time.

Based on the available evidence, it is believed that sometime during the late 1890s, John St. Helen departed Texas and moved to El Reno, Oklahoma. Here, he adopted the alias David E. George. Though unemployed, it was subsequently learned by Bates that St. Helen regularly received large amounts of money from the Booth family in Baltimore. While in El Reno, he participated in a number of theatrical productions and, by all accounts, provided excellent performances equal to the finest actors of the day. He particularly excelled in performances of *Hamlet* and *Richard III*, known to be Booth's favorite plays.

In April 1900, George, suffering severe depression, swallowed a large amount of prescription drugs and was convinced he would soon die. While still barely conscious, George told a Miss Young that he had a confession to make. He told her that he had killed "one of the best men who had ever lived, Abraham Lincoln." George asked Miss Young to bring him a pen and paper. When she did, he scribbled, "I am going to die before the sun goes down." He signed it "J. Wilkes Booth."

George recovered from his suicide attempt and several weeks later moved to Enid, Oklahoma, sixty-two miles to the north. He resided in a room at the Grand Hotel and earned his living as a part-time handyman and house painter. George was known around Enid as an alcoholic and perhaps a drug addict since he regularly took morphine.

George, as did John St. Helen, dressed in the manner of Booth, wearing a "black semi-dress style of suit of the best fabrics, always with the turned down Byron collar and dark tie . . . tailor made, new, and well pressed, his pants well creased. His shoes were patent leather and his hat a black Stetson derby." George, like Booth, was known to drink heavily and would occasionally launch into extended soliloquies and poetry. He was well educated and apparently quite intimate with the works of Shakespeare. It was learned that, in 1902, Blanche de Bar Booth, daughter of John's brother Junius Brutus Booth, paid George a visit in Enid.

On the morning of January 13, 1903, George made another suicide attempt, and this time he was successful. He swallowed a large amount of strychnine and died a short time afterward.

Then living in Memphis, Tennessee, Finis Bates read a strange article about a man named David E. George who died in Enid, Oklahoma, who some believed was John Wilkes Booth. Bates wondered if George might be the man he knew in Granbury, Texas, as John St. Helen. Bates heard that, since no one claimed the body of the deceased, it had been placed in a storeroom until such time as it could be disposed of one way or another. Bates departed Memphis and on arriving in Enid went to view the body. According to Bates, George and St. Helen were the same man.

As the years passed since the death of David E. George aka John St. Helen aka John Wilkes Booth, a series of investigations have added to the accumulating evidence that the three were the same man.

Finis Bates took possession of the cadaver, and in time, the desiccated remains essentially became a mummy. The mummy, in turn, was subjected to a fascinating journey that ranged from being displayed in carnivals as "The Assassin of Abraham Lincoln" to being studied by medical and forensic experts.

One of the studies involved a comparison of the physical aspects of the David E. George mummy versus Booth. The only officially recognized study of the day for such was the Bertillon examination, which evaluated the features of George and Booth. A number of compelling similarities were found. The test involved sitting and standing height, length of the outstretched arms, length and breadth of the head, the length of the right ear, as well as scars, eye color, and other features. Although imperfect, the Bertillon test concluded that the shape of George's head, specifically the structure of the forehead as well as the contour of the face around the eyes and the jawline, bore a striking resemblance to Booth. The analysis also revealed that the structure of the nose, particularly the bridge, the indenture of George's left nostril, and the distance from nose to mouth bore some resemblance to Booth's. Other features described by the analysis included a cocked right eyebrow manifested by both men, the ears, and the striking similarity of their hands.

George, according to Bates, bore the marks of a broken right leg. It was presumed by many that when Booth leaped from the president's box at Ford's Theater, he broke his left leg upon landing on the stage. Others who examined the body, however, stated they found no evidence of a break at all.

In 1932, Clarence True Wilson, a physician, conducted a "thorough study" of the George-Booth similarities and was convinced they were one and the same man. Over the years, Bates showed photographs of David E. George to a number of old friends of the famous actor/assassin. In each and every case, they identified the image in the photographs as John Wilkes Booth.

Another particularly telling piece of evidence involved Booth's signet ring, a piece of jewelry he was seldom seen without. The ring, sporting the initials "JWB" in bold letters across the face, was not found on the body of the man killed at Garrett's barn but was commonly seen on the finger of David E. George. George told Finis Bates that, on spotting the approach of two law enforcement officers, he feared that he would be identified. He pulled the ring from his finger, placed it in his mouth, and accidentally swallowed it. In 1931, the mummy of George was being examined by a group of seven physicians at Chicago's Northwestern University when an astounding discovery was made—a signet ring embedded in the flesh of the body cavity. It had been somewhat modified as a result of the action of digestive juices, but the initials "JWB" could be discerned on its face. In the summary of the analysis, the medical team wrote that they could safely state that the body they worked on was that of John Wilkes Booth.

CHAPTER 6

Outlaw Sam Bass and the Missing Gold Coins

The legendary Sam Bass was one of several notorious outlaws who operated out of the state of Texas during the last half of the nineteenth century. Following a series of daring holdups and the accumulation of thousands of dollars in coins and jewelry, the famed outlaw buried his wealth in four different caches in Denton County. One of these caches has been found, but where the remainder are located remains a Texas mystery.

Like those of many famous outlaws, the story of Sam Bass mixes legend with fact, but there are enough documented accounts related to his escapades to validate his reputation as a cunning and efficient outlaw, a clever and successful robber, and a man who hoarded what eventually became well over one million dollars in stolen gold coins and jewelry.

Bass was born in Indiana in 1851. Orphaned early, he was passed from relative to relative and forced to work long days on the various farms on which he lived. At eighteen years of age, Bass was determined to escape from the toil and grind of plowing, planting, and tilling. He had heard tales of opportunities that existed in Texas, as well as accounts of cowboys and ranching and adventure. Bass dreamt nightly of traveling to Texas and becoming a cowboy. One day, he packed what few belongings he possessed and struck out for the Lone Star State.

Bass arrived in Denton County in 1870, having turned nineteen on his journey. A strapping young man not afraid of hard

Sam Bass

work, Bass found a job on a local ranch and learned horsemanship and livestock-handling. At first he was thrilled with riding and roping and leading the life of a working cowboy, but the daily tedium of tending cattle soon bored him, and he sought more creative outlets.

Bass soon found work with a Denton freight company owned and operated by the county sheriff. He began hauling freight throughout North Texas and as a result came to know the countryside, the trails, and the people. A charming young man, Bass readily made friends with all he met.

During this time, Bass developed an intense interest in horse racing and often squandered his earnings betting on competitions. In time, he acquired his own racing mare and began to travel the countryside betting his horse against others. His travels took him into East Texas and parts of Oklahoma. After several months of racing and betting, Bass's winnings were handsome.

Joel Collins, a friend of Bass's from his cowboying days, talked the future outlaw into investing his winnings in a herd of cattle. Bass did so, and the two men combined their herds and arranged to drive them to Dodge City, Kansas, where they expected to sell them and make a keen profit.

By the time the young cattlemen arrived at Dodge City, however, the market had taken a turn for the worse. Discouraged and undecided as to what to do, the two decided to kill some time in a Dodge City tavern one afternoon. There, they learned that top dollar was being paid for beef in Deadwood, Dakota Territory, five hundred miles to the north. Deadwood was the center of a huge gold mining boom, and the citizens were paying high prices for fresh meat. Several weeks later, Bass and Collins arrived at Deadwood, where the cattle were sold for a decent profit.

After many months on the trail and with their pockets heavy with money, Bass and Collins paid off their drovers and began what turned into a long and expensive celebration. Their night on the town included a great deal of drinking and gambling, and before the sun rose the next morning, the two men had managed to spend almost all the money they had earned from the sale of their cattle. Disgusted with themselves, Bass and Collins began to wonder how they were going to get back to Texas.

After several fruitless days of looking for work in Deadwood, Bass and Collins were completely broke. In desperation, they decided to rob a stagecoach. Enlisting the help of three other men who were also down on their luck, they spent the next six weeks holding up stagecoaches near Deadwood.

Robbing stages turned out to be easy, and before long Bass and Collins sought greater challenges. Bass considered robbing the bank at Deadwood but decided that security was too strong. The gang drifted south looking for easier prey. They occasionally robbed stagecoaches and travelers along the way and eventually arrived at Big Springs, Nebraska.

The Union Pacific Railroad ran through Big Springs, and this gave Bass an idea—he decided to rob a train. On arriving in town, the gang rode toward the railroad station. Hiding in a grove of trees just beyond the building, the outlaws watched as the eastbound train pulled in. When the crew was distracted with filling the water tanks, the outlaws struck.

Wearing masks, the five men rode up to the train crew, leveled their revolvers at them, and forced them to open the locked door of the express car. To their delight, the outlaws found a payroll trunk containing three thousand freshly minted twenty-dollar gold pieces, each bearing the date 1877.

After loading the gold onto the horses, Bass and his gang systematically robbed all of the passengers, taking money, watches, and jewelry. This done, the gang mounted up and rode off into the night.

After they had ridden for almost an hour, the outlaws halted and divided the loot. Bass suggested they split up to confuse any pursuers, and within minutes each of the bandits was riding off in a different direction, each heavily weighted down with a share of the gold and other robbery loot.

Bass, with his saddlebags filled with a fortune in gold coins and jewelry, set his sights for Texas. On arriving back in Denton County, he learned that his friend Collins had been captured by law enforcement officials in Nebraska and subsequently shot and killed. Twenty-five thousand dollars' worth of gold coins and jewelry were found in Collins's saddlebags and returned to the railroad.

Because of the newness of the coins and the fact that each bore an 1877 date, Bass feared they could be easy to identify. He decided it would be foolish to begin spending them right away, so he cached the entire amount, intending to return for it in the future, when detection would be less likely. It is believed that Bass buried his fortune in four separate caches in the hideout he established at Cove Hollow, a relatively isolated area surrounded by dense forest and brush and located thirty miles from the town of Denton. The caches, according to Bass, were located close to one another.

Within days, Bass organized another gang that robbed stage-coaches in the area. As the stage companies grew more wary and added more guards, Bass decided to turn to robbing trains. The truth is, Sam Bass introduced train robbery to Texas; he was the first in a long line of notorious Texas train robbers. In a span of six weeks, Bass and his gang robbed four trains, all within a few miles of Denton. During one of the robberies, he was identified, and his image soon appeared on wanted posters throughout the area.

Many are convinced that after Bass committed a robbery, he carried his share of the loot to his Cove Hollow hideout and added it to one or more of his caches of gold coins. In time, he must have amassed an impressive fortune.

Frustrated with the successful repeated robberies by Bass and his gang, the railroad companies decided to call in the Texas Rangers. It wasn't long before the Rangers began to close in on the outlaws. As pursuit increased, Bass decided to abandon the Denton area and led his gang of train robbers south into Central Texas. Since the railroads had been alerted to his depredations and fortified their payroll shipments with armed guards, Bass decided to shift his pattern and rob a bank.

Bass began preparing to rob the Williamson County Bank at the settlement of Round Rock, located twenty miles north of Austin. Unknown to him, one of his gang members, James Murphey (sometimes spelled Murphy), tipped off the Rangers. A force of Texas Rangers arrived in Round Rock one day ahead of Bass and set a trap. It was reported that, as the outlaw and two of his men rode up to the bank, a number of Rangers opened fire and a brief gun battle ensued. One member of the gang was killed during the initial fusillade. Bass was seriously wounded and fell from his horse during his escape. In severe pain and with great difficulty, he managed to climb back onto his mount and flee. The third member of the gang escaped unharmed.

The Texas Rangers tracked the wounded and bleeding Bass the next morning and found him seated beneath a tree, bleeding to death. They tied him to a horse and returned him to Round Rock, where he died a short time later on his twenty-seventh birthday.

With the death of Sam Bass, people began to wonder about the vast wealth it was believed he had accumulated from his train and stagecoach robberies and cached in a secret location. Some who sympathized with the outlaw claimed that he had given most of the money to the poor and needy. This Robin Hood image has often been attributed to Bass and has some basis in fact; he was known to help the underprivileged. There were also people who regarded Bass as nothing more than a ruthless outlaw who gambled away much of the loot he stole. Despite the two conflicting claims, most are convinced that Bass buried the bulk of his wealth in separate caches somewhere in Cove Hollow.

Sometime during the first decade of the 1900s, a farmer named Henry Chapman found what many believe was part of the Sam Bass treasure. Chapman owned a small farm near Springtown in Williamson County. One day as he was riding through the woods between Clear Fork Creek and Salt Creek, Chapman's mule began acting contrary. The farmer dismounted to check the cinch on the balky animal, and as he was tightening it, he noticed a low mound of dirt a few feet off the trail. At first, Chapman believed it to be a grave, but closer examination revealed it was not. Curious, the farmer dug into the mound and was soon surprised to discover what he later described as a bushel-sized wooden box filled to the top with gold coins. All of the coins bore the mint date of 1877. When word of Chapman's discovery got around, most were convinced he had stumbled upon one of Sam Bass's treasure caches. Dozens of hopeful fortune hunters flocked to Cove Hollow to search for the others, but, as far as is known, none were successful. Except for the cache found by Chapman, none of the rest of Bass's 1877 coins ever appeared in circulation, supporting the belief that the remainder of his treasure is still buried intact.

The remaining three caches of gold coins, as well as some jewelry, likely still lie in the ground somewhere in Cove Hollow near an old trail that winds between Clear Fork Creek and Salt Creek. If found, it is estimated that the value of the three caches would amount to several million dollars.

LOST AND BURIED
TREASURE

CHAPTER 7

The Shafter Lake Treasure

Forty-three miles north-northwest of Odessa, Texas, and near the southern limits of the Texas Panhandle lies an unimposing body of water with the formal name of Shafter Lake. Technically, it is not a lake but a *playa*—a shallow depression in the generally flat landscape that fills with water during rains and associated runoff. The term *playa* is a Spanish word and has several meanings, including: "an area of flat, dried up land, especially a desert basin from which water evaporates quickly," "a dry lake," and "beach." Due to the high evaporation rates in this part of the Texas high plains, water does not remain in the shallow basin for long. After the water has evaporated, the exposed bed of the playa is covered with either salt or alkaline deposits.

The longest portion of Shafter Lake extends in a south-west-northeast direction and extends slightly less than two miles in length. At its widest, it approaches one and a quarter miles. During a normal wet year, the lake is rarely more than four feet deep.

What remains significant about this *playa* is that somewhere near the middle, there are two wagonloads of gold that sank into the soft bottom sediments during a military expedition following the Civil War, and the gold was never recovered. The value of the gold is estimated to be worth hundreds of millions of dollars in today's values.

Following the end of the Civil War, a number of Union army officers were assigned duty in the expanding frontier of the United States. Around the same time, many citizens who were displaced as a result of the war flocked into the West at an increasing rate, eager to undertake ranching, farming, and mining ventures. They were soon followed by entrepreneurs, developers, and others who sought to establish towns with schools, churches, and businesses.

Difficulty arose when the lands sought by the newcomers were occupied by a number of different American Indian tribes, some of whom had lived there for multiple generations. In seeking to defend their traditional ranges, the Indians waged war on the new settlers, and the results were often bloody. Soon, the growing demands for protection against attack were heeded by the US government. Military forts and outposts were quickly established and fortified with contingents of soldiers. Vast areas were patrolled by cavalry units in an attempt to bring order and peace.

William Rufus Shafter enlisted in the army of the North soon after the outbreak of the Civil War. By the time he reached his twenty-sixth birthday, he had accumulated battle experience at Ball's Bluff, Fair Oaks, Nashville, Yorktown, and West Point. A fearless fighter, Shafter was wounded several times, twice decorated, and won the praise and admiration of General George Henry Thomas, known to his troops as the Rock of Chickamauga. In recognition of Shafter's achievements during the war, Thomas presented him the command of a large contingent of black troopers, called buffalo soldiers by the Indians, and assigned him to frontier Texas. Shortly after arriving at his post, Shafter earned a reputation as a courageous and indomitable leader who rode into battle without hesitation and who won the respect of his troops. During Shafter's time in West Texas, he earned the nickname "Pecos Bill."

In 1957, a researcher examining a collection of military documents from the 1860s and 1870s housed in a Fort Bliss, Texas, depository encountered a cryptic report pertaining to Shafter and a contingent of soldiers escorting two wagonloads of gold from the Mexican border to some unidentified destination farther north. The year was 1875. Each wagon was pulled by a team of four mules. The source of the gold was not indicated and remains a mystery to this day. In addition, it was not specified whether the gold was in the form of ore, ingots, or coins, and an estimate of its value was never recorded. It is easy to assume, however, that "two wagonloads of gold" represent a substantial amount, perhaps several hundred pounds, and thus worth many millions of dollars today.

The paucity of information regarding this gold shipment has led some researchers to suggest that Shafter may have acquired it illegally and intended it for his own use. Staunch supporters of Shafter have taken issue with this view and resent what they consider to be a slur upon the officer's good character. Shafter advocates have offered the explanation that it was more likely that he was on a secret mission for the US government and that the gold was being transported to the US Treasury in Denver. The problem with this theory is that Shafter and his column of troopers were traveling toward the northeast, whereas Denver lay to the northwest.

Whatever the truth of the matter, the gold never reached any intended destination and lies today beneath the bottom of a dry lakebed in Andrews County on the high plains of West Texas, a playa known today as Shafter Lake.

Shafter Lake is located eight and one-half miles northwest of the town of Andrews, population 13,500. The lake is one of hundreds of such depressions that dot the Texas Panhandle. They vary in size; some amount to no more than tiny ponds, while others are often regarded as legitimate lakes by nearby residents. These playas are normally filled with saline-laden waters from runoff generated by the infrequent rains that visit this part of the country. The often intense heat of the region, along with the low relative humidity, facilitates rapid evaporation of the playa waters, leaving behind crusty accumulations of salt. Shafter Lake is one such playa and remains dry throughout much of a year and often for several years in a row.

It is known that Shafter, leading his contingent of mounted troopers along with the two wagonloads of gold, had passed two miles east of the small town of Monahans and was traveling in a northeasterly direction, when one of his scouts informed him that a band of forty Comanches was following a short distance behind. Outnumbered and well aware of the danger represented by this tribe, Shafter ordered six sharpshooters to the rear of the caravan. Their presence, he hoped, would deter any attack planned by the raiders.

Throughout the day, the Comanches remained a mile behind the soldiers, neither advancing nor making overt threats. A few minutes before sundown, the soldiers arrived at a small spring located not far from the present-day town of Notrees, twenty-five miles northwest of Monahans. Here, Shafter ordered a halt, instructed the men to set up camp, and posted a double guard around the perimeter. Few of the soldiers slept that night as they peered into the darkness looking for any sign of the Comanches they knew were lurking a short distance away.

The troopers were up before dawn the following day and, after a hasty cold breakfast, continued on the trail northwestward. As the rising sun illuminated the flat plains, the soldiers could see the Indians a mile behind them, still dogging their trail.

Travel was slow owing to the sand-choked route and occasional deep washes and gullies across which the troopers were forced to negotiate the heavily laden wagons. Three more days passed, and the party finally made camp one evening near the southwestern shore of a large playa.

Several soldiers filled barrels of water from the shallow lake to replenish what had been used during the journey, but they soon found it too salty to drink. They contented themselves with a bath, the first they'd had in several days. As they cleansed themselves, they noted that the lake was only two to three feet deep.

That evening as Shafter and his troopers ate supper, one of the lieutenants who had been studying the lake decided they would make better time by traveling across it rather than going around it. Though he had not investigated it to any degree, the lieutenant insisted that the lake bottom was firm enough to support horses, mules, and wagons. Shafter accepted the recommendation, a decision he would come to regret.

The next morning, the troopers dined once again on a cold breakfast, hitched the mule teams to the wagons, and mounted up. Moments later, Shafter motioned the column forward and into the playa, his intention being to avoid the long route around the body of water. The Comanches, now within a half mile of the soldiers, were no doubt pleased with Shafter's decision. The Indians were familiar with this, as well as dozens of other playas in the region, and were well aware of the real and potential threat to horses and wagons presented by the soft, muddy bottom.

The initial several dozen yards of the crossing were uneventful. As the column entered the deeper section of the lake, the saline waters lapped at the boots of the riders and the wagon bottoms, but progress was no slower than what they had grown accustomed to over the past several days. As the party neared the middle of the lake, however, trouble began. The lead pair of mules on the first wagon became bogged down in the soft sands and silts and were unable to proceed. As the troopers worked to free them, the trailing pair also began sinking, soon followed by the wagon itself. Within ten minutes, the first wagon, bearing its heavy weight of gold, had vanished below the surface of the water. In addition, the second wagon, along with the mule team, was slowly sinking into the saturated sands and silts of the lake bottom. Extra horses and mules were brought in and harnessed to the wagons but to no avail. They, too, sank into the mud and drowned.

As the struggle to save the gold-laden wagons continued, more and more horses became mired and were struggling to extricate themselves from the mud. Several troopers were forced to abandon their mounts and alternately swam and waded their way to the northeastern shore. It was apparent that the gold had been lost, and the entire contingent of soldiers was in disarray.

As Shafter watched the futile efforts to save the wagons and the gold, the Comanches arrived at the south end of the lake. Forming a single line stretched out along the shore, they remained mounted while observing the frantic activities of the troopers. When it became clear that their quarry was in a somewhat defense-less position, the leader of the tribe issued a loud cry, sending his armed warriors into the lake toward the confused cavalrymen.

After regarding the approaching Comanches for a moment, Shafter ordered his disorganized men to abandon the wagons and make their way toward the northeast shore of the playa. On reach-ing their objective, the cavalrymen did not stop but continued their frantic flight from the pursuing Indians across the plains. Many of those who lost their horses to the muck at the bottom of the playa fled on foot; others were pulled onto already mounted horses and rode double.

The Indians chased the troopers for four miles before reining up. Returning to the mired wagons and animals near the middle of the lake, they found little that was useful, save for some harnesses, ropes, and sheets of canvas. Careful to avoid being trapped in the soft, muddy bottom, the Indians secured these items and rode back toward the southwest. Shafter and his men, grateful to have survived the confrontation with the Comanches, continued to whatever destination was originally intended. The greatest loss, of course, was the hundreds of pounds of gold in the two wagons that had sunk into the soft muds at the bottom of the playa.

Except for small bands of Indians and occasional travelers, this part of West Texas was seldom visited during those few years following the Civil War. As a result, the two wagons and their loads of gold caught in the shallow playa bed went unnoticed for decades. Over time, the wooden planks of the wagons fell into rot, spilling the shipments of gold onto the lakebed. The heavy weight and high density of the gold caused it to sink deeper into the soft, saturated sands of the playa.

According to existing records, Shafter and his command never ventured back to the dry lake to retrieve the gold in the body of water that now bears his name. Military assignments kept him occupied elsewhere. One of his assignments was to lead a company of cavalry on the island of Cuba during the Santiago campaign in 1898. Shafter passed away in 1906. As surveys were made throughout West Texas and maps drawn, the body of water eight and one-half miles northwest of the town of Andrews was named after William Rufus Shafter, the military leader who is credited in US Army documents as having "discovered" it.

During the early 1900s, the southern Panhandle of West Texas experienced a land boom. As a result, an area businessman named J. F. Bustin founded a town on the north shore of Shafter Lake. The original name of the town was Salt Lake, but it was later renamed Shafter Lake after the adjacent body of water. By 1907, Shafter Lake had evolved into a rather thriving village with businesses, over fifty homes, a post office, churches, a school, and a newspaper. By 1910, the population was estimated to be five hundred residents. In time, a contest developed between Shafter Lake and nearby Andrews for the title of county seat. After a county election, Shafter Lake lost to Andrews by only a few votes. By 1912, most of Shafter Lake's residents had moved to Andrews.

Today, all that remains of the town of Shafter Lake is the old cemetery of twelve graves and one original building. The land where the town once thrived is now a ranch operated by the descendants of Shafter Lake's first postmaster.

For over a century, few, if any, were aware of the fortune in gold lying somewhere in the sand, silts, and salts that make up the bottom of Shafter Lake. Were it not for the discovery of documents that described Shafter's journey, the flight from the Comanches, the difficulties encountered in crossing the playa, and the loss of millions of dollars' worth of gold, the event would remain hidden in the dusty archives of history.

The found government documents are compelling, but after the passage of nearly a century and a half, a dedicated investigator requires more evidence before undertaking a search for the lost treasure. Evidence of such an event in what was at the time a remote part of West Texas would seem hard to come by, but dogged research paid off with the discovery of supporting verification.

During the summer of 1901, a few pieces of rotten wagon timber were found near the middle of a dry playa bed in West Texas by a man named William Russell. Russell, along with his wife and three children, were traveling from Denton, Texas, to Pecos, when their wagon broke down near a dry lakebed northwest of Andrews. Russell set up camp, and while he and his wife made repairs on the wagon, his two sons explored the crusty surface of the playa.

Later that day during the evening meal, Russell noticed that one of his sons was playing with some items he had never before seen. When he examined them, Russell realized they were harness and wagon fittings. When Russell asked his son where he found them, the boy pointed toward the middle of the nearby playa and stated that they were lying on the surface.

The next morning before continuing with repairs on the wagon, Russell walked out onto the playa. Near the middle, he discovered the rusted and rotted remains of at least two wagons, as well as some weathered bones of horses and mules. Unaware of the saga of William Shafter's scrape with the Comanches and the lost treasure, Russell wondered how the wagons and mules came to be in the middle of the dry lake. As he looked around the area, Russell had no way of knowing that only a few inches to a few feet below where he was standing resided a fortune in gold.

Russell completed repairs on his wagon and proceeded on to Pecos, where he eventually established a successful commercial orchard and truck garden. Approximately ten years after settling in the small West Texas town, Russell told a friend about finding pieces of wagons out on the dry lakebed near Andrews. The friend related a story, one he heard from a former black cavalryman who had served under William Shafter. The ex-trooper told about two wagonloads of gold that had sunk into the lake and had to be abandoned because of an Indian attack.

Russell was excited about the possibility of returning to the playa and retrieving what he knew must be an amazing fortune. After all, he had seen the remains of the wagons and mules and knew the location where they had become mired in the lake. Several weeks later, Russell, along with his two sons, now grown, traveled by wagon to the playa now known throughout the region as Shafter Lake. On arriving, however, they found it filled with water to a depth of three feet, the result of recent rains and runoff in the region. Russell and his sons remained encamped on the shore of the lake for several days while he attempted to formulate some strategy relative to retrieving the gold. Finally, he gave up and returned to Pecos. Russell made several more trips to Shafter Lake but each time found it filled with water.

In 1931, an unnamed ranch hand told a story in Andrews that generated some level of excitement. The ranch hand stated that while he was out searching for some stray cattle two weeks earlier, he was crossing a dry lakebed northwest of town when he found several pieces of an old wagon scattered across several yards of the playa. Two ranchers who overheard the story were familiar with the tale of Pecos Bill Shafter's lost gold and traveled out to the playa the next morning. The day, as well as the previous week, was particularly windy, and by the time they reached the dry lakebed, they found it largely covered by a thin layer of sand blown in by the strong West Texas winds. Though they searched for several hours for the remains of the wagons, they found nothing.

As far as anyone knows, the two wagonloads of gold that sank into the bottom muck of Shafter Lake in 1875 are still there. Given today's technology and equipment, there is a distinct possibility that it can be located and recovered. But there are obstacles to confront and overcome.

The first obstacle facing the hunter of the lost Shafter Lake treasure relates to the size of the area to be searched. Though the shoreline has changed a bit over the past century and more, the playa is approximately two and a half square miles in extent. This is quite a bit of ground to cover, but it is possible to whittle the search area down. The military documents related to the event refer to the wagons becoming mired "near the middle of the lake." In addition, William Russell and the unnamed ranch hand both referred to finding wagon parts "near the middle of the lake." This narrows the search area somewhat, but it must be remembered that "near the middle of the lake" is only a relative location and one that could include an area several dozen square yards in extent.

Another obstacle is related to water. As previously stated, Shafter Lake is occasionally all or partially filled with water at various times during the year, depending on the occurrence and intensity of area rainfall. In order to facilitate a search for the treasure, it would certainly be easier if it took place while the lakebed is dry.

A third obstacle to consider is the real or potential depth of the treasure. When Shafter Lake is filled with water following heavy rains, the porous sand and silt of the bottom becomes saturated and expands, turning into a variety of quicksand. Heavy objects can easily sink into the soft, loosely consolidated substrate. Gold, as well as silver, lead, and some other precious metals with relatively heavy weight and high specific density, will easily and effectively sink into such a saturated environment. In one recorded instance, silver ingots, after having been tossed into a river that had a bottom similar to that of Shafter Lake, had sunk to a depth of as much as eight feet. With regard to the playa, it is a distinct possibility that the heavy gold has long since sunk deep into the soft bottom of the lake.

The depth that the gold has potentially sunk will be a function of the depth of bedrock. This can be determined by examining geology maps and descriptions of the area. Or perhaps a government soil conservation employee would know.

For the sake of argument, let's assume the gold has sunk to depth of eight feet. To determine the exact location, one would need to have access to a high-quality, state-of-the-art metal detector or ground-penetrating radar. These are easily obtained. Once the location and depth of the sunken gold has been determined, one may very well find it necessary to obtain and employ a backhoe in order to pursue the excavation. If the gold is no more than two or three feet, shovels may suffice. If deeper, a backhoe will facilitate the recovery.

Today, Shafter Lake is no longer the semi-remote location it was as recently as sixty years ago. As of 2019, hundreds of gas and oil wells have been drilled within a half mile of the lake, and petroleum company vehicles and employees are ubiquitous throughout the area day and night. An excavation conducted in search of the Shafter Lake treasure would not go unnoticed. In fact, as of 2019, there were at least six gas wells *in* the lakebed. Before one undertakes an excavation, one would need to determine how it would be affected by the nearby gas and oil leases, as well as the possibility that the playa itself is likely to be private property leased to the drilling company.

For a century and a half, the Shafter Lake treasure has eluded the handful of searchers who learned of the account and arrived in the area. Because the treasure is relatively unknown to most, it has not been sought like many higher-profile treasures, such as those associated with the Superstition Mountains of Arizona, Nova Scotia's Oak Island, and the Lost Adams Diggings long believed to be located in New Mexico. That the Shafter Lake treasure exists is, based on the extant military documents that refer to it, a foregone conclusion. The exact location of the treasure within the limits of the playa yet needs to be determined as well as a realistic plan for recovering it.

CHAPTER 8

The Goatherder's Lost Treasure

A fortune in gold and silver coins has lain in a remote cave in the Guadalupe Mountains of West Texas for over a century and a half. The cache was likely robbery loot taken from an Overland Mail stagecoach and hidden by person or persons unknown. The treasure was accidentally found sometime during the 1930s then lost. Searchers have come and gone over the decades, but the location of this hoard remains elusive. If found today, it would be worth many millions of dollars.

During the time before paved roads and the development of small settlements and ranches in the region of the Guadalupe Mountains, located 110 miles east of El Paso, Texas, the native grasses found there were rich and plentiful, once described as growing "hip-high to a tall horse." Because of these nutritious grasses, the region was deemed to be ideal for the raising of livestock. Soon, several small cattle, sheep, and goat ranching operations were established along the foothills and plains that stretched out and away from the impressive escarpment.

During the early part of the twentieth century, a man named J. C. Hunter arrived in this area and saw the front slope of these mountains with its rich grasses as having great potential. A short time later, Hunter purchased several thousand acres of land from the foothills deep into the mountain range and moved in large herds of Angora goats. At this time, mohair was in great demand. Mohair is the yarn made from the long, silky hair of this goat, and those who could keep the eastern markets supplied with this commodity were making huge profits. Soon, Hunter's successful goat ranching enterprise in the Guadalupe Mountains had proven him correct, and he made good money in the mohair market.

In time, Hunter's ranch became one of the most successful in the region. In addition to goats, it was stocked with cattle and sheep. Hunter employed several cowhands, as well as a number of sheep and goatherders. One of the goatherders who worked for Hunter was a young man named Jesus Duran, who preferred to be called by his nickname—Jesse. Jesse, along with his parents and siblings, had migrated from somewhere deep in the Mexican state of Coahuila to Texas two years earlier. After crossing the Rio Grande, Jesse went looking for employment, a search that took him to the Hunter ranch in the Guadalupe Mountains. Jesse brought with him years of experience from herding goats in Mexico. Hunter gave him the responsibility of tending a large herd of goats, which fed on the nutritious grasses along the southeastern slope of the range.

Jesse was described as an uncomplicated and uneducated youth. He had never learned to read or write but was a good, dependable worker. He never owned anything of value during his lifetime. With his job on the Hunter ranch, his basic needs for food and shelter were satisfied. Though he earned a small salary, Jesse had little need for money and sent most of his wages to his parents, who had settled in Laredo, Texas. By anyone's standards, Jesse Duran lived in relative poverty, but one day during the spring of 1930, he discovered a cache of great wealth in a small cave in the mountains, a discovery that was to change his life and set in motion a series of searches for treasure that continues to this day.

Jesse was tending his goat herd early that spring morning on the top of and along the flanks of Rader Ridge, a long, narrow limestone prominence that juts out from the southeast-facing slope of the Guadalupes and extends toward the El Paso–Carlsbad highway, less than a mile distant. For two days, a light rain fell on the region, accompanied by a brisk wind. Jesse wrapped his woolen poncho tightly around his shoulders and watched his goats from the sparse protection of a juniper tree. When he noticed his canteen was empty, he decided to hike over to Juniper Spring to fill it.

Juniper Spring was a mile southwest and downhill from Jesse's location. He rose, turned into the wind, and struck out for the water source. After a few minutes of walking along the narrow goat trail, Jesse decided to take a shortcut across the limestone slope. The new route proved to be somewhat rougher. Large table-size slabs of limestone lay everywhere, and Jesse soon found himself walking around and atop them. Once, as he stepped onto a rain-slicked slab of rock, it gave way under him and slid down the slope for several feet, spilling the goatherder to the ground.

As Jesse rose and wiped the mud from his pants and poncho, he noticed a small opening in the limestone outcrop where the large rock had previously rested. In the dim light of the overcast morning, he bent low, peered into the dark space, and realized he was staring into a shallow cave. As his eyes grew accustomed to the dark interior, Jesse recoiled in surprise at what he saw.

Just inside the opening, propped up in seated positions against the right-hand wall, were three skeletons. What little remained of clothing hung loosely from the bones. Leaning against the opposite wall were three rifles.

As he stared into the cave, Jesse saw something else that gave him pause. On the floor of the small cavern just beyond the skeletons were three strongboxes, the kind used by Wells, Fargo and the Butterfield Overland Mail company to transport valuable cargo. One of the boxes was open, and Jesse saw that it was filled nearly to the top with gold and silver coins.

Frightened, Jesse touched nothing in the cave and dared not pass through the entrance. With difficulty, he replaced the heavy limestone slab over the opening. He hurried on to Juniper Spring and filled his canteen then returned to his herd on the ridge and pondered what to do about his discovery.

Late in the day, Jesse decided what his next move must be. He believed it was his responsibility to inform the Hunter ranch foreman of what he had found. Making certain the goats were secure, he walked several miles to the home of Frank Stogden, arriving one hour past sundown. Mrs. Stogden greeted Jesse at the back door and invited him in out of the cold and rain for some coffee. She told Jess that Stogden and three neighboring ranchers were playing cards in another room and would see him as soon as they were finished.

An hour later, Stogden summoned Jesse. He and the other three cowboys listened as the young Mexican related the story of his fascinating discovery. Stogden and his friends were ready to ride out to Rader Ridge and retrieve the treasure immediately, but Jesse was hesitant. He told the men that he feared the spirits of the dead that resided in the cave. He explained that Mexicans believed in the concept of *El Patron*, a life-force that watches over hidden treasure and protects it from those who are not worthy of possessing it. Jesse was a devout Catholic with a strong belief in the powers of departed souls. He said that to enter the cave and disturb the site by removing the treasure would anger the spirits and bring hardship, even death, to the perpetrators and their families. Jesse told the men that he believed nothing but evil would result from a return to the treasure cave.

The cowmen questioned Jesse for the next hour about the location of the cave, but the young herder's fears made him cautious and reluctant, and they did not want to risk further refusal. The men finally agreed to wait until morning to continue discussing the matter. Stogden invited Jesse to spend the night in the barn. In the morning, he said, they would all ride out to Rader Ridge and examine the cave. By dawn, however, Jesse Duran was gone. He was never seen again in the vicinity of the Guadalupe Mountains.

Following breakfast the following day, Stogden and his three companions saddled their horses and rode to the base of the south-facing slope of Rader Ridge, arriving around midmorning. They reached Juniper Spring, dismounted, tied off their horses to nearby trees, and undertook a search of the area on foot. The rain of the previous days had obliterated any sign of Jesse's presence.

According to an interview with Stogden many years later, the ranch foreman stated that Jesse insisted he found the small cave while hiking downslope from Rader Ridge toward the spring. Leaving the old goat trail, Jesse had walked several yards along an exposed limestone ledge when he slipped on the large, flat rock. Jesse told Stogden that when he was standing in front of the cave, he was no more than a quarter of a mile from Juniper Spring.

Stogden and his friends searched for the location all day but found nothing. They encountered dozens of flat limestone slabs, large and small. Together, they lifted one heavy stone after another to one side, hoping to locate a small cave beneath, but found nothing. After searching for most of the day, they gave up and returned to their respective homes. The four men visited the area off and on over the next several months looking for the cave, but after successive failures, they eventually abandoned the search.

In time, others learned of the story of Jesse Duran and the elusive treasure cave. Soon, the foothills of the Guadalupe Mountains between Rader Ridge and Juniper Spring were swarming with men eager to find the cache, but like Stogden and his neighbors, they had no success.

Extensive research into the tale of Jesse Duran suggests that the treasure cache did, indeed, exist and in all probability consisted of chests of gold and silver coins most likely taken during one or more robberies of the Butterfield Overland Mail coaches that traveled the road through Guadalupe Pass, a short distance downslope from

Guadalupe Mountains

the spring. The loot, presumably cached by the robbers in the small cave, was never retrieved.

The massive limestone reef that is the Guadalupe Mountains extends for nearly two hundred miles and transects the Texas–New Mexico border. Within these mountains can be found hundreds of caves. One, Lechuguilla Cave, is considered to be the largest cavern system in the world. Not far from Lechuguilla Cave is the famous Carlsbad Caverns, a national park. This region is also pockmarked with smaller caves, some just barely large enough for a man to crawl into. Most extend only a few feet into the bedrock. Within a mile of Juniper Spring can be found several of these smaller caves.

At one time, the Butterfield Overland Mail route passed less than a mile south of Juniper Spring. The Pinery, a stage stop where the horses were fed, watered, and rested, is located two miles to the southwest of the spring. During its brief existence, the stage line transported passengers as well as mail, money, and supplies. The line also carried shipments of gold and silver from mines in the West to brokers, banks, companies, and individuals in the East.

It is a fact that desperadoes lurked in the remote canyons of the Guadalupe Mountains and that the outlaws sometimes stopped coaches as they labored up the steep grade toward the Pinery Station and robbed them. Records show that the coaches were halted, passengers robbed, and chests containing gold and silver coins were taken on several occasions.

Given this blending of facts, along with the Wells Fargo–style chests seen by Jesse Duran, it is not unreasonable to conclude that the cave stumbled upon by the goatherder served as a cache site for items stolen from the stage line. It is more difficult to explain the presence of the three skeletons Jesse claimed he saw in the cave. Perhaps they were victims of the robbers. Or maybe there was a disagreement over the division of loot, and three of their members were killed and left in the cave.

Other strongboxes and chests have been found in the Guadalupe Mountains, all documented. In some instances, the perpetrators of the robbery and caching were captured or killed or otherwise denied the opportunity to return to the hiding place to retrieve the stolen goods.

A few skeptics have questioned the veracity of Jesse Duran's tale, suggesting that the young goatherder made it all up. Old timers in the area of the Guadalupe Mountains who claimed to have known Jesse all stated that he was an honest, sincere, trustworthy, and hard-working young man who was not inclined to make up stories. He was well liked and had the respect of all who knew him.

In researching what became of Jesse Duran, it was learned that, after fleeing foreman Stogden's residence that night, he went to the home of his sister in Carlsbad, New Mexico, sixty miles to the northeast. There, he remained in hiding for three months, rarely leaving the house. According to his relatives, Jesse's fear of *El Patron* was so strong that he continued to believe that his accidental discovery of the treasure might bring bad luck to his family. At the first opportunity, he left his sister's home and traveled to California. There, Jesse worked as a farm laborer until his death in the early 1970s.

Evidence exists that others may have found the treasure on the side of Rader Ridge, but they were unaware of the significance of their discovery. Sam Hughes ran a successful cattle and sheep ranch in Dog Canyon, located on the north side of the Guadalupe Mountains. One day Hughes was deer hunting with several friends near Juniper Spring when he claimed he accidentally slipped on a large slab of limestone and fell, landing partially in the opening of a small cave. Fearing that rattlesnakes might be residing within, he quickly extracted himself and continued with his hunt. At the time, Hughes was unaware of the story of Jesse Duran's lost treasure cave.

That evening, as Hughes and his friends were relating the day's activities around the campfire, the rancher told of his fall into the cave. Noel Kincaid, who replaced Stogden as the foreman of the J. C. Hunter ranch and an occasional searcher for the treasure himself, asked Hughes to describe the cave and its location. The description of the small hole matched the one Jesse Duran provided years earlier. Hughes also said the cave was approximately one-quarter of a mile northeast of Juniper Spring. The following morning, the deer hunters returned to the area to search for the cave but were unable to relocate it.

Lester White was a white-bearded, sun-wrinkled outdoorsman who lived in and around the Guadalupe Mountains, mostly in temporary camps, cooking his meals on an open campfire. White was a throwback to the days of the grizzled and tenacious prospectors who lived for that one big strike. In this case, White searched for lost mines and buried treasures throughout the Guadalupe Mountains.

White had spent fifteen years in the range off and on, but he had never heard the story of Jesse Duran's lost treasure cave. One evening, while seated around a campfire, a visitor told him the tale of the skeletons and rifles and of the chests filled with gold and silver coins. White responded by saying that he may have encountered that very cave a few days before but was unaware of what lay inside.

White told of a time when he was exploring an area about one mile northeast of the old rock house that served as the headquarters for the Hunter ranch and where foreman Noel Kincaid lived at the time. White said he was not far from Juniper Spring when he encountered a small cave quite by accident while he was resting near an old goat trail that led from the spring to the top of Rader Ridge. He said that at a point just below where he sat, he detected the opening of a small cave partially concealed by a large, flat limestone slab. Curious, White climbed down to the location to inspect it. According to his statement, the rock had slid a few inches downslope, thus exposing a portion of the cave opening beneath it. White said it had appeared as though someone had placed the rock over the cave in the past with the intention of hiding the entrance.

White climbed down to the location and peered into the hole through the tiny space between the slab and a corner of the opening. What he saw caused, he said, "the hair on the back of my neck to stiffen." Inside the cave, White saw "at least two skeletons and a bunch of rotted cloth." White had encountered skeletons in caves in the range in the past but paid little attention to them. Most of them were clearly Indian burials, and he chose to leave them alone. He presumed that this most recent discovery may have been one such burial, and he was determined to allow the location the respect he felt it deserved. Carefully, White adjusted the limestone slab such that it recovered the opening and resumed his explorations.

On hearing the story attributed to Jesse Duran, White became convinced he had found the treasure cave but had mistaken it for something else. White assured his visitor he could relocate the cave, and the following morning, the two men hiked over to Juniper Spring. From the spring, White confidently led his friend in a northeasterly direction along the rugged, rocky slope of Rader Ridge, his thoughts on the great fortune he was convinced he was going to retrieve from the small, remote cave.

Arriving at a limestone outcrop, White paused and scanned the immediate area carefully, stating that the place looked different on this morning than it did on the evening when he was there days earlier. Flat limestone slabs littered the area, and White could not determine which of them was the one he had replaced over the opening. He and his companion shifted several of them to one side but found no cave. Here and there small holes and slightly larger openings into shallow caves could be seen. All were examined but nothing was found.

The two men searched the slope, stopping only now and then for a sip of water from a canteen. By dusk, White, dejected, decided it was time to give up. For months afterward, he returned to the area and searched for that one particular limestone slab that covered the provocative opening to what he was convinced was the treasure cave. He never found it. Lester White searched off and on for the elusive cave until he passed away sometime during the 1970s.

Like Lester White, others have arrived at this location over the years in search of Jesse Duran's lost treasure cave. Thus far, the treasure has not been found.

Today, the area around Juniper Spring lies within the boundaries of Guadalupe Mountains National Park. The spring, as well as Rader Ridge, is far from any authorized hiking trail. The park service discourages any off-trail exploring, though it happens from time to time. Though hunting for lost treasure is forbidden on federal lands, hopeful fortune seekers still occasionally make their way to Juniper Spring to undertake their search for the goatherder's lost treasure cave.

CHAPTER 9

Lavaca River Treasure

Of all the pirates who sailed the Gulf of Mexico off the Texas coast, none garnered more recognition than the colorful, dashing, and daring Jean Lafitte. Although dozens of such brigands plied the gulf waters attacking ships and raiding coastal communities, most of their names are lost to history. Jean Lafitte was the outlaw buccaneer most associated with the coast of Texas—the Jesse James of the open sea.

Much of what has been written about Jean Lafitte over the years has been consigned to legend, but many of his exploits, as well as his buried treasures, have been documented. Jean Lafitte was indeed noteworthy and notorious, and he left behind rich treasures in gold, silver, jewels, and precious stones. (Although the pirate was born Jean Laffite [2 fs, 1 t] allegedly in France, most English language documents and resources spell his surname "Lafitte" with 1 f and 2 ts. Since that remains the most common usage, that is the spelling that will be used here.)

Despite intensive research into the origins of Jean Lafitte, much of his early life remains a mystery. During at least one point in his life, Lafitte claimed to have been born in Bordeaux, France, in 1780. His parents, he said, were Sephardic Jews whose ancestors fled Spain for France during the 1760s. On another occasion, Lafitte, along with his brother, Pierre, claimed to have been born in the French city of Bayonne. Research into Lafitte's background has

Jean Lafitte

yielded additional claims that he was born in the French towns of Brest and St. Malo. One of Lafitte's biographers, however, suggests that it was convenient to claim France as a birthplace during his time for it provided some element of protection from American law. Yet other accounts provide Orduna, Spain, as well as Westchester, New York, as his place of origin.

To add to the confusion of Lafitte's origins, author Jack C. Ramsey introduces the notion that the pirate was born in the French colony of Saint-Domingue, the former name of present-day Haiti. A number of French plantation owners migrated from Haiti to Louisiana, where they established expansive farms. An examination of population records of Haiti from the 1760s reveals a number of families with the surname "Lafitte" living there. Ramsey suggests that Lafitte, along with his brother and widowed mother, left Saint-Domingue for New Orleans in the 1780s.

Another Lafitte biographer—William C. Davis—claims Jean Lafitte was born in Pauillac, France, in 1782, one of nine children. Davis also claims Pierre was Jean's half-brother. According to Davis, Lafitte's father was a trader who owned ships and spent much of his time at sea and that the young Jean learned his seamanship by serving aboard those vessels.

It is known that, as a young man, Lafitte was fascinated with the bayou country of Louisiana and spent days exploring as much of it as possible. In time, this interest led to the exploration of inlets, harbors, and other locations eastward onto the Mississippi coast and westward along the Texas coast. While Jean was learning much about the geography of the Gulf Coast, his older brother, Pierre, was operating as a privateer out of Saint-Domingue. A privateer referred to an individual who held a government commission authorizing the use of his vessel in war, especially in the capture of enemy merchant shipping. The vessel itself was also called a privateer. Evidence suggests that Pierre brought captured merchandise to New Orleans to sell and that he was assisted in this endeavor by his brother, Jean.

By 1812, Jean Lafitte had grown tired of his role as a broker of stolen cargo. He saw some advantage in capturing the cargo himself and eliminating the middleman. With that in mind, he and Pierre purchased a schooner and employed a man named Trey Cook to captain it. As the schooner did not apply for a commission from the government, it was therefore operating illegally. According to the law, such a vessel was regarded as a pirate ship.

In January 1813, the Lafitte brothers captured a Spanish slave ship. They later sold the slaves in Louisiana, along with some of the additional cargo, and pocketed eighteen thousand dollars. The brothers converted the slave ship into a pirate vessel and named it the *Dorada* after a Mediterranean fish. After capturing another ship using the *Dorada,* the Lafittes deemed it a less than useful pirate vessel and returned it to its owners. As a pirate, Lafitte gained the reputation as a gentleman. He always treated captured crewmen well and freed them at the first opportunity. Seized goods were taken back to New Orleans and sold.

Thomas B. Robertson, the acting governor of Louisiana, had grown perturbed by the piracy activities of the Lafitte brothers. While the residents of the Louisiana coast appreciated the Lafittes for providing them with goods at a low cost, Robertson referred to them as "brigands who infest our coast and overrun our country." When Governor William C. C. Claiborne returned to office and sent Robertson back to his previous duties, he relaxed the official pressure on the Lafittes.

On June 18, 1812, the United States declared war on Great Britain. The US, however, was at a naval disadvantage. While Great Britain had a powerful navy, the US had only a few ships. In order to fortify the navy, the US government offered letters of marque to private vessels. A letter of marque authorized a private citizen, a privateer, to attack and capture enemy vessels and bring them before admiralty courts for possession and sale. One such letter was granted Jean Lafitte. While Lafitte turned over some of the captured booty to the authorities, most of it was sold illegally through his and Pierre's operation. When this became clear to the authorities, and they realized how much revenue they were losing from Lafitte's illegal activities, they set out to prevent him from continuing.

On November 10, 1812, US District Attorney John R. Grimes filed charges against Lafitte for "violation of revenue law." Three days later, Jean and Pierre Lafitte were captured along with twenty-five of their crewmen. Contraband was confiscated, but while the authorities were distracted, the Lafittes escaped.

In March 1813, Jean Lafitte registered as the captain of a sailing vessel, a brig. While he listed his job as piloting the ship on a trip to New York, he was, in truth, once again establishing himself as a privateer. Not long afterward, he obtained a letter of marque from the country of Colombia. Although he captured ships and seized cargo, he never returned any of it to Cartagena in northern

Colombia, directing it instead to the port of New Orleans, where he and brother Pierre continued to sell it.

This blatant disregard for Louisiana laws angered Governor Claiborne, who began making plans to recapture the bandits. He appointed his revenue officers to prepare an ambush. In addition, a five hundred dollar reward was offered for the capture of Jean Lafitte. In return, Lafitte had dozens of handbills printed up to hand out and tack up on walls that offered a five hundred dollar reward for the governor.

In January 1814, Lafitte arranged for an auction of a large amount of contraband outside of New Orleans. Federal authorities attempted to break up the operation, and in the process one of the revenue officers was killed and two others wounded. In addition to these difficulties, New Orleans merchants were putting pressure on the governor to do something about Lafitte because the pirate was charging lower prices for the same goods. Claiborne responded to the ongoing difficulties by approaching the state legislature and requesting approval to establish a militia company to remove the pirates from Louisiana once and for all. The legislature appointed a committee to study the matter, but the truth was that they were in no hurry to roust Lafitte, as many of their constituents benefited from the pirate's sales of goods. A short time later, Pierre Lafitte was arrested, convicted, and jailed on charges related to acts of piracy.

The jailing and conviction of Pierre did not deter Jean one whit. While his brother was incarcerated, Jean operated the piracy and smuggling business with impunity. In response to Lafitte, as well as other pirates, the British navy increased patrols through-out the Gulf of Mexico. In August 1814, they had established a naval base at Pensacola. In September, a British ship fired on one of Lafitte's vessels and gave pursuit. Lafitte took to shallow water, where the larger British ship could not follow. The British commander raised a white flag and indicated that he wanted to talk. He had a dinghy lowered into which several officers took seats and rowed toward Lafitte's ship. Lafitte likewise lowered a rowboat and went out to meet them halfway.

The captain of the British ship, Nicholas Lockyer, along with Royal Marine Infantry Captain John McWilliam (sometimes spelled with one l), had been transporting a package with orders to deliver it to Lafitte. Lafitte invited the men to row to the nearby island. On arriving at the island, the officers were surrounded by Lafitte's men as the pirate identified himself to them. They handed over the package.

Inside was a letter from King George III, who offered Lafitte and his pirates full British citizenship as well as land grants in the British colonies in the Americas if they promised to assist in the naval fight against the United States. The letter stated that if Lafitte refused, they would bombard Barataria, a known pirate haven south of New Orleans and a base of operations for Lafitte. The second letter was from Lieutenant Colonel Edward Nicholls of the Royal Marines urging the pirate to accept the offer.

Lafitte realized that, regarding his operation in Barataria Bay, he would eventually have to fight either the US or the British. He felt that he had a better chance of eventually succeeding against the US forces later, so he decided to align with the British for the time being. But Lafitte then sent a message to US officials informing them that some of his men wanted to side with the British, but that they would side with the American forces if Pierre was released. The offer was accepted.

On September 13, 1814, US Navy Commodore Daniel Patterson led a warship, six gunboats, and a tender into Barataria Bay and began shelling ships and the settlements on the shore. Ten of the pirate ships formed a battle line in the bay and returned fire, but it became clear that the US forces were winning. Lafitte, realizing the outcome of the battle, ordered his men to abandon the ships. Several of the vessels were set afire. When Patterson's troopers arrived on the shore, they met no resistance, took eighty captives, captured eight pirate ships, $500,000 worth of stolen goods, but could not locate Lafitte, who had escaped into the nearby forests and swamps.

Governor Claiborne wrote letters to US Attorney General Richard Rush and General Andrew Jackson requesting a pardon for the Baratarians and implied that Commodore Patterson had erred in destroying the "first line of defense for Louisiana."

In mid-December 1814, Andrew Jackson arrived in New Orleans and met with Jean Lafitte. Lafitte offered to help defend New Orleans against the British if the United States would pardon any of his men who agreed to join in the fight. Jackson, the only person who could issue pardons, consented to the terms, and on December 19, the state legislature recommended a full pardon. Encouraged by Lafitte, many of them joined the New Orleans militia or volunteered to serve as sailors on the ships. The rest formed three artillery companies.

On December 23, several ships of the British fleet sailed up the Mississippi River toward New Orleans. Lafitte noted that the

American line of defense did not extend far enough to keep the British from encircling the American troops. Lafitte told Jackson it was necessary to extend the line into the swamps, and Jackson gave the order to do so. The British commenced firing on the Americans on December 28, but were driven off by an artillery company manned by two of Lafitte's former lieutenants.

During the ensuing battles, Lafitte's men distinguished themselves in helping defeat the British. Even Jackson voiced praise for the bravery and skill of the former pirates. With Jackson's recommendation and the legislature's recommendation, the US government granted full pardons to Jean and Pierre Lafitte as well as all of the men who had served under them. Pardons were granted on February 6, 1815.

It was only a matter of time before Jean Lafitte made his way to Texas. During his pirating activities, Lafitte had been taken with the Texas Gulf Coast and the potential opportunities for establishing a pirate colony. In January 1816, Jean and Pierre Lafitte made an agreement with Spain to serve as spies. At the time, Spain was involved in a war with Mexico, which was fighting for independence, and Texas belonged to Spain. Jean was ordered to Galveston Island on the Texas Gulf Coast. Galveston served as a headquarters for the pirate Louis-Michel Aury, a French privateer who sympathized with the Mexican ideals. During March or April 1817, Lafitte displaced Aury and assumed command of Galveston Island. Lafitte found the island ideal for his needs: It was essentially uninhabited save for his own men and the Karankawa Indians, and it was outside the authority of the United States. He lost no time in establishing it as a base for his smuggling operations. Lafitte's crewmen tore down the house constructed by Aury and built dozens of new ones for the officers and crew, along with storage facilities.

Before 1817 ended, Lafitte's Galveston Island colony, which he called Campeche, boasted a population of almost two hundred men and women. Newcomers to the island were required to sign a loyalty oath to the pirate. Lafitte remained busy attacking and capturing merchant and slave ships. The Galveston Island location served Lafitte well until a series of mishaps took place. After some of his men kidnapped a Karankawa woman, the Indians attacked the colony and killed five men. Lafitte's gunboats rained fire on the Karankawa encampment, killing most of the inhabitants. Not long afterward, a hurricane devastated the island; most of the houses were destroyed, along with several ships. Lafitte continued to use the island as a base from time to time, but it was never the same.

In 1820, Lafitte reportedly married Madeline Regaud, the daughter of a French colonist. They had a son—Jean Pierre Lafitte. In 1821, the USS *Enterprise* was ordered to Galveston Island to remove Lafitte and his pirates once and for all in response to an attack on an American merchant ship. Lafitte met with the captain of the *Enterprise*, a man named Kearney. After several days of discussions and negotiations between the pirate and Kearny, in the hope that this would appease the captain, Lafitte ordered the hanging of two men he said were responsible for the attack on the American ship. Kearney was not impressed with Lafitte's gesture. He instructed his sailors to aim the guns of the *Enterprise* toward the island and gave Lafitte thirty days to vacate. Lafitte agreed to depart without a fight. Lafitte decided to shift his operations to Matagorda Bay, one hundred miles to the southwest.

Several days before the period was to expire, one of Lafitte's ships, the *Pride,* was somehow forced aground near the mouth of the Lavaca River deep in Matagorda Bay, one hundred miles down-coast from Galveston Island. Lafitte was not on board at the time. A number of hull planks were fractured, and the vessel sank in the shallow waters. The *Pride* was known to have been carrying a great quantity of treasure taken during raids of several Spanish ships in the Gulf of Mexico. Lafitte, in the company of a number of crewmen, sailed to the site and recovered a wooden chest filled with a treasure of gold and silver coins as well as jewelry, along with two canvas sacks containing a number of silver ingots. The booty was carried to shore. After dividing much of it among his crew, Lafitte assigned two men to ready the remainder for caching. Lafitte and his men hauled the treasure several hundred yards across the salt marsh, selected a suitable location, and buried it in a shallow hole.

Lafitte took a compass reading and a bearing on two nearby mottes, or groves of trees growing atop a low mound—Kentucky Motte and Mauldin Motte. The pirate made notes in his journal, and when he was finished, he took a long brass rod he had carried from the ship and shoved it deep into the ground of the marsh adjacent to the treasure, until only eight inches remained visible. Lafitte then told his two companions that if they returned to the site after three years and found the treasure still there, they could have it. This done, Lafitte sailed back to Galveston Island.

Before vacating the island, Lafitte and his men burned all of the standing structures and buried most of the stolen cargo. Several of the crewmen were later arrested and convicted of piracy. Those who were not captured joined Lafitte aboard one of his ships. When Lafitte informed them he was returning to piracy, half of the men refused to accompany him. He allowed them to depart and told them they could take his other ship, the *General Victoria*. That night, Lafitte, apparently in a vengeful mood, led his pirates aboard the *General Victoria*, where they crippled the ship by destroying the masts and spars. And then Lafitte sailed away, never to return to Galveston Island or Texas.

For the next several months, Lafitte preyed on Spanish ships in the Gulf of Mexico. When he had filled his hold with stolen cargo, he returned to the barrier islands near New Orleans, where he would unload it and replenish his supplies. Brother Pierre handled the sales of the contraband. As this was going on, the congressional delegation of Louisiana petitioned the federal government to do something about Lafitte and put an end to his piracy and smuggling. In response, ships from the US Navy were sent to the Gulf.

During the ensuing weeks, a number of pirates had been put out of commission. In November 1821, Lafitte was fired upon, pursued, and captured. On February 13, 1822, he escaped. Once free, Lafitte acquired more ships and established a pirate base on the island of Cuba, after bribing local elected officials. In April, as he set his sights on seizing an American merchant ship, he was captured again. This time the Americans turned him over to the Cuban authorities—hoping they would be responsible for him—who promptly released him.

Lafitte continued to prey on ships in the Caribbean. Unfortunately, several of the ships he captured and pillaged were carrying important and necessary goods to Cuba. This angered Cuban officials, who sought to put an end to Lafitte's depredations. With the increased pressure from the Cubans, Lafitte arranged with Colombia to raid Spanish ships.

On February 4, 1823, Lafitte's ship engaged in a battle with two Spanish merchant vessels. The Spaniards were heavily armed and inflicted great damage to the pirate ship. During the onslaught, Lafitte was severely wounded. According to reports, he died on the morning of February 5 and was buried at sea. In spite of this account, the death of pirate Lafitte is beset with mystery. Some reports have him meeting his end in the Yucatan. Others place him in Honduras. And yet another has Lafitte abandoning his piratical ways and fleeing to Indian Territory (Oklahoma), where he lived under an alias. According to researchers, Lafitte never returned to recover the treasure buried near the mouth of the Lavaca River.

Lafitte has been gone for a long time, but the treasures he cached in various locations, many believe, are yet to be found. With regard to the Lavaca River treasure, according to legend, one of his trusted companions who helped him cache it died from malaria within a few months of Lafitte's departure from the island. Before he died, however, he related the account of the burial to a friend. Using the directions provided by the late pirate, the friend made several unsuccessful trips to locate the chest and the silver ingots.

The second pirate who assisted with the burial of the treasure never returned to the site, choosing instead to remain in New

Orleans and raise a family As an old man, the former buccaneer told the story of the buried chest of gold and jewels to his two sons. With great enthusiasm and certain of their ability to find the treasure, the sons organized an expedition to the Lavaca River marsh, but they, too, failed to find it.

More time passed, and a man named Hill sought to establish a ranch on the land located at the junction of the Lavaca River and Matagorda Bay. He stocked the grassy marshes with fine horses and cattle. One of Hill's employees was a black farmhand named Ward, who was placed in charge of the livestock. Ward's responsibilities included running horses and cattle out into the marsh during the day to graze and returning them to the pens each night.

While the livestock were grazing in the marsh during the day, Ward would sometimes lay down on the grassy sward and take a nap. One afternoon as he was tending the stock on horseback, he grew drowsy and searched for a good spot to stretch out on the soft ground. Dismounting, he looked around for something to which he could tie his horse. Nearby, he found the tip of a brass rod sticking out of the ground. After hitching the horse to the rod, Ward lay down a few paces away and dozed off.

The horse Ward was using on this day was unaccustomed to being staked. He pulled at the rod, bending it and extracting almost its entire length. When Ward awoke from his nap, he pulled the rod completely out of the ground and carried it back with him when he returned with the stock, intending to show it to his employer.

Rancher Hill was familiar with the tale of Jean Lafitte's buried treasure, and when he saw the long brass rod, he knew it immediately for what it was. Hill told Ward he wanted to be taken the next morning to the spot in the marsh where the rod was found. The two men searched throughout the area the following day, but Ward was unable to relocate the spot where he had lain down to nap.

In 1870, a man was turkey hunting near the mouth of the Lavaca River. On spotting a flock of birds several dozen yards away, he got down on his hands and knees and crawled toward his quarry. As he was slowly creeping along on all fours, the turkey hunter's knee struck hard against something partially buried in the ground. When he turned to examine what it was, he saw what he thought was a low pile of small bricks. Wondering why bricks would be in this remote location, he placed one in his pouch, intending to examine it later.

On returning home, the hunter removed the heavy brick from the pouch and showed it to his brother. The brother scratched the surface of the object with his penknife and discovered it was an ingot of almost pure silver. Familiar with the story of the pirate Lafitte, the turkey hunter deduced he had stumbled onto a portion of the lost pirate cache.

When the brothers sought the location of the pile of silver the following day, they could not find it. Though the two men searched several miles of the grassy marsh, the sameness of the region throughout its extent made it difficult to pinpoint any specific location. They searched in the area of Kentucky Motte and Mauldin Motte, but neither man was aware of the relationship of the mottes to the treasure cache.

Another man may have actually found Lafitte's treasure cache, but it seems likely that he only removed a few gold coins from it. A rather eccentric local resident known as Crazy Ben was familiar to most residents in the Galveston Island area, but he was seldom taken seriously and remained unfriendly to all. The old man was never known to hold down a job, and he lived in squalor in an old shack. What distinguished Crazy Ben from other area residents was the fact that he paid for his drinks with gold Spanish coins.

Crazy Ben often told the story of when he served as a cabin boy to the pirate Jean Lafitte and that he secretly followed the famous buccaneer and his two crewmen across the salt marsh and watched as they buried the chest filled with treasure and the sacks of silver ingots before returning to Galveston Island. When the pirates left the area several days later, Ben, no more than ten years old at the time, remained, living in a shack on the south bank of Clear Creek near Galveston Bay, working as a fisherman and handyman, and when times were lean, he begged for handouts. After several years had passed and Ben was certain that Lafitte was never going to return to retrieve his buried treasure, he traveled to the site near the Lavaca River, dug up the chest, and helped himself to a handful of coins. After pocketing the money, he reburied the chest. With the few coins in his pocket, Ben returned to Galveston and was able to live well and drink his fill for several weeks. When he finally ran out of money, he simply returned to the cache and retrieved more coins.

An unambitious man, Crazy Ben preferred to drift around the bay area visiting different taverns and spending his coins on ale. During his common alcohol-fueled conversations with fellow drinkers, Ben would admit to deriving his income from the buried treasure chest of the pirate Jean Lafitte. Word of the source of the old man's wealth spread throughout the region, and from time to time men would attempt to follow him into the marsh. Ben always managed to elude them.

One evening after a full day of drinking at a local tavern, Crazy Ben staggered out of the establishment and down the street toward his shack. Moments later, two shadowy figures left the tavern and followed him into the night. That evening was the last time anyone saw Crazy Ben alive. The following morning, his body was found washed up on the shore of Galveston Bay not far from his home. His throat had been slashed, and most believed he was killed because he would not reveal the location of the Lafitte treasure.

Other attempts to locate the Lavaca River treasure cache of Jean Lafitte have been made during the past century and a half. During the 1920s, a man arrived in the area of the Lavaca River from Oklahoma with what he claimed were the original handwritten notes from Lafitte's journal describing the location of the buried treasure chest. Although the newcomer had no trouble locating the two prominent mottes, he was unable to find the cache. The search continues.

CHAPTER 10

The Cursed Treasure of Pirate Jean Laffite

The buried treasure cache near the Lavaca River is not the only one in Texas associated with the pirate Jean Lafitte. There are, in fact, so many stories of lost treasure associated with this fascinating buccaneer that they would fill an entire book. Many of these tales are undoubtedly exaggerated and amount to nothing more than just that—tall tales. As the reputation and mystique of this daring and adventurous pirate grew, so did the number and kinds of legends and accounts associated with him, particularly those regarding buried pirate loot. In spite of the proliferation of buried treasure stories linked to Lafitte, a number of them possess tantalizing elements of truth, and deep investigation yields compelling evidence pointing to the notion that many of these treasure tales are based in fact.

Another, and important, truth is that Lafitte himself cultivated this mystique. He was an elusive, sly, and enterprising adventurer to be sure, but he was also a highly skilled self-promoter who understood the value of possessing a reputation as a notorious and feared freebooter.

One of the more intriguing and mysterious tales of Lafitte's buried treasures is one that is said to have a curse associated with it. Any who attempted to remove the treasure other than Lafitte himself, according to the curse, would be struck down and rendered helpless. As the stories go, many were, some even unto death.

Sometime during 1820, Jean Lafitte and his crew piloted a treasure-laden ship to a location near where the Neches River of Texas enters the secluded bay of Port Arthur near the Texas-Louisiana border. Steering the vessel as close to shore as possible, Lafitte selected a site to bury several chests filled with gold and silver coins and jewels recently taken from a Spanish ship on its way to Cuba. As he was searching for a suitable cache site, Lafitte was also concerned about pursuit from a second Spanish galleon, one whose captain was intent on exacting revenge on the pirates.

Lafitte had his ship moored by stretching a long, heavy iron chain to a stout tree near the river. The pirate leader then had his men bury the chests in the shadow of this same tree. After lowering the containers into the excavation, the pirates spotted the pursuing Spanish vessel sailing into the bay and began heading toward them. According to the legend, Lafitte had one of his crewmen killed, wrapped in sailcloth, and placed in the hole atop the chests. After refilling the excavation, Lafitte ordered his men back on board the pirate ship. Before leaving the cache site, however, the pirate stood over the recent excavation, raised his face to the heavens, and placed a curse on the treasure. He vowed that anyone unworthy who tried to recover the treasure would be stricken with unnamed horrors.

On returning to the ship, the pirates hoisted the sails, primed the cannons, and unfastened the heavy chain, tossing it into the water. The other end was still attached to the tree.

As the pirate ship moved out into the bay, Lafitte challenged the Spanish galleon. For over an hour, the two ships exchanged cannon fire, but it soon became clear that Lafitte's ship was getting the worst of it. Realizing this, Lafitte, wishing to avoid defeat and possible capture, eluded the Spaniards and sailed out of the bay and into the Gulf of Mexico. Lafitte's relief at escaping was short-lived for the Spanish ship fell into pursuit once again and was closing in. Approximately two miles out into the gulf, Lafitte's ship took two direct cannon hits and started to sink. Most on board went down with the vessel, but Lafitte and a few crewmen escaped and made their way back to the nearby shore. Weeks later, the pirate had obtained another ship and was back in the business of sailing the Gulf of Mexico and preying once again on Spanish merchant ships. According to the legend, Lafitte never returned to the Neches River to retrieve his treasure.

Decades later, when Jean Lafitte was just a distant memory to many Gulf Coast residents, a curious map surfaced. It was of crude construction, and, with difficulty, one could make out a description of the chaining of the pirate vessel to the tree, the burying of what was apparently millions of dollars' worth of treasure, and the subsequent battle with the Spaniards. Though inexpertly drawn, anyone familiar with the area could easily recognize the Neches River, Port Arthur, and related landmarks.

This odd map came into the possession of a Mexican peasant right after the Civil War. According to the man's widow, he followed the map, found the tree with the heavy chain still attached to it, and started digging. To this day no one knows what he found, if anything, for when he returned home the following day, he was in a state of shock and unable to speak. Whatever happened to him during his attempt to recover the treasure caused him to lose his voice. Within a week, he was dead from unknown causes. The man, it is believed by some, was the first victim of Lafitte's curse.

Several years later, the Mexican's widow passed the map on to a neighbor. A farmer with a small family, he grew excited at the prospect of locating one of Jean Lafitte's treasures. He began making plans for a trip to the mouth of the Neches River. The Mexican woman, however, did not tell the neighbor of the fate of her husband.

Using the map, the farmer, after obtaining a shovel and pickaxe, traveled to the location on the Neches River. Days later and like the man before him, the farmer found the tree with the chain attached and began excavating. According to his version of what transpired, after digging a hole approximately two feet deep, the farmer suddenly jerked upright as if seized by something unseen. He dropped the shovel, flailed his arms, and grasped at his throat, seemingly trying to ward off strangulation. With difficulty, the farmer scrambled out of the hole. After taking some time to recover, he made his way home. Like the Mexican before him, the farmer lost the ability to speak. Before the week was out, he died. All of his belongings, including the treasure map, were stored and forgotten. The farmer was the second victim of the curse.

Many years later, the farmer's widow cleaned out many of her late husband's belongings and gave them to a neighbor named Meredith, who had recently moved into the area. When Meredith asked about the old map, the widow explained what had happened to her husband when he searched for the treasure as well as what happened to the man before him and related that she believed they were both victims of Jean Lafitte's curse. Meredith thought this nothing more than mere superstition and exaggeration. He told the widow he placed little credence in curses and was highly skeptical of the tale she had related. Meredith decided he wanted to try his hand at recovering the treasure and recruited a partner, an old friend named Clawson, to assist him in the search. After studying the old map, the two men made their way to the mouth of the Neches River.

With little difficulty, Meredith and Clawson located the tree near the river. The long, heavy chain, now badly rusted, was still attached to it. Next to the tree was a shallow cavity where someone had excavated a hole years earlier. Nearby, Meredith found a weathered shovel and pickaxe.

Meredith and Clawson began to excavate at the site of the cavity. They had removed about three additional feet of soil when they encountered a skeleton carefully laid out and wrapped in what had once been sail canvas. The metal buttons and buckles along with the remains of leather boots suggested it was the skeleton of a pirate. Very carefully, the two men removed the skeleton and placed it aside with the intention of reburying it later.

As the hole deepened, Meredith and Clawson, growing tired, decided to alternate digging chores. After a stint in the hole,

Meredith climbed out and leaned against the tree for some rest as Clawson took his turn. Meredith was on the point of falling asleep when he was suddenly jarred awake by Clawson's screams. Jerking upright, Meredith saw a wide-eyed Clawson frantically scrambling out of the deep hole. He looked as if he had aged twenty years, and his eyes were wide in fright.

Clutching tightly to Meredith, the frightened and tearful Clawson begged to leave the place immediately. Meredith tried to look into the pit to see what his partner had seen, but Clawson held on to his friend and prevented him from approaching the hole. Pulling Meredith's face close to his, the quivering Clawson stated that he "had just stared into the depths of hell and seen all its horrors."

Clawson's terror was so overwhelming and his hold on Meredith so unyielding, there was nothing to do but abandon the project and leave the place at once. The men ran down the trail and away from the site, abandoning all of their tools and other equipment. When they finally arrived home the following day, the still frightened Clawson begged his friend never to return to the site of the pirate treasure.

In spite of Clawson's experience at the treasure site, Meredith returned to the site two weeks later—alone. With caution, he approached the tree and the recently excavated hole. He spotted the skeleton lying where he and Clawson had placed it earlier. The hole had been partially filled in with mud as a result of recent rains. Feeling nervous, Meredith carefully placed the skeleton back into the hole and filled it in. He gathered all the tools, departed, and never returned to the site for as long as he lived.

Clawson never completely recovered from his frightening experience. Although he did not die as did others associated with the treasure site, he lived the remainder of his life in terror, jumping at the slightest sound. He eventually moved to Beaumont, Texas. Several years later, Meredith was in Beaumont on business and looked up his old friend, Clawson. During their conversation, Meredith tried to get his friend to describe what he had seen in the treasure pit years earlier. His friend refused to discuss it and begged Meredith never to ask him again.

Whatever the Mexican, the farmer, and Clawson saw in the treasure pit may never be known. The stories have endured, passed down through the years, all the while contributing to the notion of a curse. If, indeed, such a curse was effectively placed on the huge treasure cache, it adds another dimension to the mysteries associated with the complex and elusive pirate Jean Lafitte.

In 1952, a man was hiking along the west bank of the Neches River near where it entered the Gulf of Mexico when he decided to take a break. He sat down beneath the shade of a thick-boled oak tree, sipped water from his canteen, and decided to take a short nap. Moments later, he sought to relieve some discomfort by changing positions, and when he moved, he discovered he was lying atop a partially buried metal chain, heavy with rust. Looking around, he saw that the chain had encircled the tree, the trailing end leading toward the shore and into the water of the bay. He gave the matter little thought and eventually continued his hike. Several years later, he learned the story of Jean Lafitte's cursed Neches River treasure cache and the role the chain had played during previous searches for it. Convinced he could relocate the exact tree, dig up the treasure, and become a wealthy man, he returned to the area. Though he searched off and on for days, he was never able to find the chain-encircled tree. He lost the chance to become rich, but if the tales are true, he may have sidestepped a traumatic event and even death by avoiding Jean Lafitte's curse.

CHAPTER 11

The Mystery of the
Bottomless Pit Treasure

Throughout the world, there exist a number of geographical features that have been identified as bottomless pits or bottomless lakes. These are, in truth, small openings in the earth's crust that extend to impressive depths and often fill with water. None of them, however, are truly bottomless. Such a feature does not exist.

The notion of a bottomless opening in the earth has long had a strange appeal and effect on humans. These unusual geomorphological forms possess an aura of mystery and wonder. The Bible refers to a bottomless pit as a place where demons are imprisoned. Most so-called bottomless pits and lakes are nothing more than sinkholes, some of which have filled with water. Near Roswell, New Mexico, is the Bottomless Lakes State Park, which features nine such "lakes." Each is a water-filled sinkhole, and the deepest extends no more than ninety feet. A few other locations identified as "bottomless" are nothing more than deep holes scoured out in rivers and streams as a result of the erosive action of the water.

A noted "bottomless pit" is located in Dimmit County, Texas. It is called the Grand Rock Water Hole, and the area nearby was a favored campsite for travelers for more than a century. The water hole is a large spring and has acquired a level of fame because, for generations, residents in the area have insisted that the spring is bottomless.

The Grand Rock Water Hole is additionally famous for another reason: Somewhere in its depths may lie a fortune in gold and silver coins and ingots, a treasure that is, according to legend, worth millions of dollars.

In the first decade of the nineteenth century, Texas was still a part of Mexico, and the town of San Antonio was the commercial center for this northern realm. Many wealthy Spaniards and Mexicans made San Antonio their home, and trade and travel between this burgeoning community and Mexico City were frequent. Gold and silver coins and bullion were regularly shipped from one city to the other.

Sometime during the early summer of 1893, a pack train consisting of thirty mules loaded down with millions of dollars' worth of gold and silver coins, as well as dozens of ingots of each mineral, left Mexico City bound for San Antonio. Several drivers were hired to lead the mules on the long journey north, and the pack train was accompanied by fifty well-armed Mexican soldiers intent on keeping the treasure safe from bandits and Indians that might be encountered along the way.

In charge of the party was Captain Palacio Flores. Flores was a favorite officer of Mexican general Santa Anna and came from a prominent family. A bright future was predicted for the young captain, and if he performed well on this assignment, he believed he would be considered for a promotion and a transfer to a position of authority in the capital.

The journey north was uneventful for the first portion. Passing through the beautiful mountains and plains of eastern Mexico, the party paused to rest at cities such as Celaya, San Luis Potosí, and Monterrey. They encountered neither Indians nor bandits along the way, and the pack train made excellent progress.

The route followed by the Flores-led party crossed the Rio Grande fifty miles upstream from Laredo and into the rugged, rocky, brush-covered hills of South Texas. Almost immediately, the guards spotted a dozen men on horseback observing the pack train from safe distances. Before leaving Mexico City, Flores had been warned by other soldiers who had previously traveled this road of the ruthlessness of the bandits that could be encountered here.

Nervously, the soldier guards kept scanning the horizons and ravines for any sign of the outlaws, but no attack came. It was clear, however, that the pack train was being followed, stalked.

On the first evening after crossing the Rio Grande, Flores selected a campsite and ordered the mules unloaded, with the packs of gold and silver stacked nearby and placed under a double guard. Soldiers and drivers spent an uneasy and restless night anticipating an attack from the bandits. The night passed quietly, however, and when morning came, the treasure was loaded back onto the mules, and the pack train began winding its way along a tortuous trail toward San Antonio, 120 miles to the northeast. Because of the rocky and broken ground, travel was slow. Flores, often referring to a map, made plans to establish the next camp at a location known by travelers as the Grand Rock Water Hole.

On this leg of the trip, Captain Flores noted that the number of men observing the progress of the pack train from a distance had increased to nearly thirty, in his estimate, and that they were venturing closer. Flores had a sensation that an encounter with the trackers might be growing near. He alerted his soldiers to be extra wary.

Flores and the party arrived at a stream called Peña Creek and followed it for several miles. Late on the afternoon of the second day after crossing the Rio Grande, the party rounded a sharp bend in the creek and spotted the well-known spring known as the Grand Rock Water Hole and the associated campsite several dozen yards beyond. Flores again ordered the treasure unloaded from the mules and had the drivers stack it at a location near the water hole. Flores explained to his contingent that they would remain at this location for two or three days while they and the mules rested for the final portion of the trip into San Antonio.

The welcome spring was several feet across and its depth unknown. The waters were cool and refreshing and a welcome sight to the weary travelers. They filled water barrels and took long-postponed baths.

Following the evening meal, Flores again doubled the sentries. The camp spent another fearful night, the men constantly on the alert to the possibility of an attack from the mysterious riders. All was quiet that night again, however, and throughout the entire next day, none of the bandits were spotted.

By the end of the afternoon, Flores was beginning to believe that the threat of an attack had passed, and he decided not to post extra guards over the gold and silver shipment that night. The young, inexperienced captain had convinced himself that he and his soldiers were overreacting to the presence of the riders and perhaps overrating the threat. The captain, like many of his kind, was convinced his soldiers possessed sufficient bravery and firepower to repel any kind of attack. That evening, the soldiers and drivers slept with only a handful of sentries on guard.

The following morning, as the men roused from their sleep and went about preparing breakfast, dozens of armed riders thundered out of adjacent ravines and attacked the camp. Swarming into the midst of the still drowsy soldiers and drivers, they slaughtered several as well as horses and mules. The initial attack lasted only a few short minutes. Having succeeded in their aim, the raiders turned and raced back to their hiding places in the nearby ravines and gullies to regroup and ready for the next attack, which Flores presumed would come soon. The captain immediately organized a contingent of musketeers into a skirmish line to fend off the invaders.

As the soldiers readied their weapons and strapped on their swords, Flores ordered the drivers to throw the packs of gold and silver coins and bullion into the spring. To lose the wealth entrusted to him would be to disgrace himself and jeopardize his career as a soldier. Flores intended to do all he could to keep the outlaws from taking the treasure. When the battle was over, he would recover the gold from the spring and deliver it to San Antonio. Flores, however, had no inkling as to the depth of the spring.

As Flores pondered his plan, a second rush from the bandits erupted from the ravines and resulted in the killing of several more soldiers. For the first time, Flores was beginning to fear the outcome of the battle. When the last of the packs was tossed into the clear waters of the spring, Flores himself yanked his saber from its scabbard and went to the front line to join his men in attempting to repel the invaders.

On the third and final charge into the poorly prepared and frantic swarm of soldiers, the raiders clearly dominated. Flores was killed within the first few seconds, and with their leader gone, the disoriented troopers and drivers went running in all directions seeking safety. The raiders, their lust for killing sharpened by their victory, chased down the panicked men, slaying most of them.

One of the drivers, an elderly man named Alejandro Lajero, took refuge in a dense clump of brush just beyond the outer edge of the campsite and escaped notice by the raging bandits. While the raiders fought over the choice mounts and spoils of the camp, Lajero cowered in his hiding place until dark. When he believed it was safe to do so, the old man crept out of hiding. He looked around and, spotting no survivors, moved silently through the brush and continued the journey to San Antonio alone and on foot.

Several days later, Lajero, weak and near starvation, arrived in the city and related the attack of the massacre at the Grand Rock Water Hole. Several men in authority reluctantly suggested assembling a mounted force and returning to the area to punish the bandits and recover the treasure, but it was clear they feared the outlaw element in that part of Texas and decided to wait.

As time passed, what little enthusiasm there was for returning to Grand Rock Water Hole diminished. Soon, the hidden Mexican treasure in the depths of the spring faded from the thoughts of San Antonio's authorities and residents, and with the passage of years, the deadly incident was gradually forgotten.

Decades elapsed, and the treasure of the Grand Rock Water Hole came to mind again in 1893, when a reporter for a San Antonio newspaper found several references to the event in some obscure archival material he encountered. The reporter tracked down information about to whom the gold and silver were to be delivered some ninety years earlier and contacted the descendants. Soon, the heirs organized a group to try to locate and recover the treasure.

With considerable difficulty, the search party traveled the rocky trail to the area and eventually located the Grand Rock Water Hole. They found that, despite the passage of nearly a century, the ground surrounding the spring was littered with the bleached bones of men, horses, and mules. True to the descriptions they had been provided by the reporter, the waters of the spring were cool, clear, and delicious. Try as they might, however, they could not plumb the bottom of the pool.

The searchers used long poles to probe but were unable to contact the bottom. Two members of the party volunteered to dive to the bottom, but after several attempts stated that the waters went far beyond the depths a man could go. Tying ropes together and weighting one end with a large rock, they lowered the line deep into the pool to a depth of well over one hundred feet but never touched bottom. The search party eventually decided to give up and return to San Antonio. In the telling of their experience at Grand Rock Water Hole, they referred to the location as a bottomless pit, a term that stuck and was thereafter used to describe the location of the treasure. Though the subject was discussed several times, the group undertook no further efforts to try to retrieve the treasure, a fortune in gold and silver coins and ingots that lay at the bottom of the water hole.

According to researchers who have investigated the accounts related to the Grand Rock Water Hole treasure, now referred to as the Bottomless Pit treasure, the spring was located on a bank near Peña Creek in Dimmit County and a few miles northwest of the town of Carrizo Springs. Some area residents claimed that over the years the spring has run dry. Others insist that it filled with silt in earlier years from the creek's flooding. Still others claim that the spring exists just as it did when Captain Flores and his soldiers camped there and that somewhere far below the surface of the cool blue water lies a great fortune in gold and silver.

HAUNTINGS

CHAPTER 12

The Devil on the Border

The devil is perceived in a variety of ways by the world's different cultures. Traditionally, as a result of interpretations by many religions, the devil is the personification of evil; the objectification of a hostile and destructive force. Historically, the concept of the devil braids elements of theology, mythology, psychiatry, and even art and literature. In Christianity, the devil, or Satan, is regarded as a fallen angel and serves the role as an opponent of God.

To many, the devil is little more than a myth, a subject for folktales, and is not taken particularly seriously. To others, however, the devil is real, powerful, always tempting us, and an entity to be avoided. Few places on earth is the devil regarded as earnestly as he is in the town of Presidio, Texas, and in Ojinaga, its sister city across the Rio Grande. In these locations, his alleged presence has maintained a mysterious hold on these communities for centuries, since the time of the earliest Spanish settlement in the region.

On first reading, the following story appears to possess the elements of a folktale. To a large degree, it is that, for certain, and is largely dismissed by the skeptical. But the skeptics do not live in Presidio or Ojinaga and have not seen and experienced what the residents of the region have. To those affected, and there have been many, the devil is entirely real, and belief in him and his terrors has been passionately embraced for hundreds of years clear up to the present day.

Presidio, Texas, is a town with a population of 4,500 and is located immediately north of the Rio Grande across from the Mexican town of Ojinaga. It is a point where the Conchos River flows out of Mexico and confluences with the Rio Grande. Most of the water in the Rio Grande from this point on to the Gulf of Mexico comes from the contribution of the flow from the Conchos River.

More than three centuries ago, this area represented a significant crossroads and stopping place for travelers, mostly Spanish adventurers, coming north out of Mexico on the Chihuahua Trail. The concept of a border as we know it today did not exist then, and Presidio and Ojinaga functioned as a single large community, one with a river flowing through the middle. The two towns together were referred to as *La Junta*, the Junction.

Prior to the arrival of the Spaniards, this region was occupied by as many as two thousand Indians. The indigens lived in earthen houses and were primarily agriculturalists, planting on and harvesting their crops from the fertile floodplain of the Rio Grande. Interaction between the Indians and the Spanish explorers was common, and in time the government authorities in Mexico City recommended the establishment of a mission at La Junta. Its purpose would be to serve the Spaniards who frequented the region but also to convert the Indians to Christianity. Into this setting arrived a parish priest by the name of Urbano. (Different historical accounts give his name as Gomez, Pedro, and Urbán.)

Father Urbano met with difficulty shortly after his arrival at La Junta, for it turned out that his domain was beleaguered by the devil himself. The devil, according to those who related the stories to the priest, lived in a cave in a nearby low mountain range. Some versions of the tale locate the mountain range south of the river. Others have it just north of the present-day town of Presidio, and still others insist that it is in a small range located east of the town.

The devil has long had an influence on this region of Texas in more ways than one. A significant number of geologic and geographic landforms bear his name: Devil's River, Devil's Lake, Devil's Ridge, Devil's Backbone, Sierra Diablo, Diablo Plateau, and more.

According to the stories passed down over the years, the devil routinely emerged from his cave to terrorize the inhabitants of La Junta. Sometimes the devil would appear to the Indians who were working in the agricultural fields, dancing lewdly in front of them and making frightening faces. Other times he could be seen racing up and down the valley floor, smashing everything he came in contact with. On the occasions when the river dried up and the lack of water caused the crops to wither, the devil was blamed. Only prayer, along with contributions to the church, claimed Father Urbano, would cause the situation to get better.

Even worse, according to the priest, the devil infected the morals of the town's inhabitants. At night, it was said, the devil entered the homes of the unwary and whispered evil thoughts and desires into their ears and hearts. He was responsible, wrote chronicler Elton Miles, for infidelity, for the rebellion of children against their parents, and for murder. Father Urbano clearly had his hands full in dealing with this sinister force.

The devil that haunted Presidio was seen and described by many. He reportedly walked upright like a man but on legs that resembled those of a rooster, including the spurs on his heels. He was known to have taken young girls off into the night, their bodies found the next morning, torn and bloody. Father Urbano decided something must be done.

The priest ordered the construction of a wooden cross, one that was six feet tall but made of wood light enough so it could easily be carried. Father Urbano named it the *Santa Cruz*, the Holy Cross, and dedicated it to the task of driving the devil from the area. Initially, the cross seemed to exert no influence whatsoever over the devil one way or another. Despondent over the continued reign of the evil spirit, the parishioners refused to attend church. Father Urbano decided he must confront the devil himself.

Alone, the priest walked to the reputed lair of the devil in the mountain range. He was undecided as to what to do, what to say to this fearsome entity. By the time he reached the base of the slope, he was still in a state of confusion. He stared up at the crest of the range where the devil's cave was located and began to climb. The trek to the top was rugged and dangerous at places. Halfway to the top and on the edge of a steep cliff, Father Urbano encountered a stranger on the trail ahead of him. The priest described him as "dressed in black," and the man "leered at him with dagger-point eyes." The stranger asked the priest what he was doing on the mountain and what was his destination.

Father Urbano replied that he was concerned for his people. Once, he said, they were all good folk, hard workers, and dedicated church-goers, all with fine families. Now, said the priest, all they do is drink, gamble, steal, philander, and possess no respect for the commandments of God. Further, many of them have ceased attending holy mass. Father Urbano told the stranger that it was none other than the devil who inserted his evil ways into the hearts and minds of the poor Indians.

The stranger, in turn, expressed sympathy and then related specific incidences of robbery, murder, infidelity, and lying among the citizens of La Junta, even providing the names of those guilty of such. Stunned and suspicious, the priest regarded the stranger anew and asked who he was and how he came to have this information.

"I am the devil!" boasted the stranger, laughing. "I, along with my rebellious companions, were evicted from heaven. As we fell toward the earth, forever to be in exile, I tried to think of a place where I would want to live."

The devil pointed toward the peak and said, "I found this place, this desolate mountain where I decided to make my home in a cave up yonder, and I have lived here ever since. Every night, I visit the town and whisper into the ears of your people. I tell them what I want them to do, and I tell them to pay no attention to you. In this, priest, I am succeeding."

In a rage, the priest advanced on the devil, holding the Holy Cross up above his head and flailing at him with his fist. In his flight from the priest, the devil slipped and fell from the high cliff, screaming all the way to the valley floor below. At first, Father Urbano thought the devil was vanquished, but after a moment, he saw him rise from the ground and scramble back up the side of the mountain to confront the priest. Once again, advancing on the devil with the cross held before him, the priest forced the demon to retreat all the way to his cave. As the devil screamed from within the darkness of his sanctuary, Father Urbano thrust the base of the cross into the ground at the entrance, believing that it would keep the devil forever imprisoned within.

Father Urbano raced down the mountain and back to the town. There, he assembled his parishioners and explained what he had done. He provided instructions for what was to happen next.

The following day, the priest led his faithful parishioners back up the mountain to the devil's lair. Atop the peak just above the cave of the devil and using the rocks they found, they erected a shrine. From the woods along the river, they cut and carried four-inch-thick logs for rafters. Cane was laid across them and topped with earth to form a substantial roof. Against one inside wall of the shrine, the priest placed the Holy Cross so that "it might stand forever as a charm to keep the devil in his cave below."

The mountain was given the name *El Cerrito de la Santa Cruz* ("the Little Hill of the Holy Cross"). To this day, the cave just below the shrine is known as *La Cueva del Diablo* (the Cave of the Devil).

Afterward, back at La Junta, the people filled the church, confessed their sins, and did penance at the shrine on the mountain. Once again, the river flowed full and strong, and healthy crops grew from the fields.

The victory of Father Urbano over the devil was revered to the point of establishing an annual ritual to celebrate the event. It is called *El Día de la Santa Cruz* (Holy Cross Day) and continues to be celebrated to this day. For years, two days before the special event, the men and boys from the town gathered brush and firewood and carried it, along with kerosene, to construct bonfires on the sides of the trail leading to the cave. The brush piles were lined up along the trail from the mouth of the cave down to the river. This done, a priest would walk the trail, sprinkling holy water on the brush piles. On the evening before Holy Cross Day, the fires were lit. In town, the citizens fired guns, beat on pots and pans, and yelled loudly to frighten the devil so that it would never appear again.

In recent times, on Holy Cross Day, a priest carrying the Holy Cross and followed by a procession would walk the fields blessing the crops and praying for bountiful yields of cotton, corn, beans, and melons and for a strong flow of water in the river. Following this, the cross was returned to its position in the shrine on the mountain.

During the past several decades, the fires have not been lit along the trail from the mouth of the cave to the valley below during the celebration of Holy Cross Day due to fewer participants. Today, there are three crosses in the shrine. On the commemoration day, they are removed, carried down the mountain and across the fields. They remain there until May 17, when they are returned to the shrine.

The celebration of Holy Cross Day is gradually dying out, the younger members of the population less influenced by the real and potential threat of evil than were their parents, grandparents, and great-grandparents. It has also been reported that church attendance is down. On Halloween, however, the fires are still lit near the cave in the belief that it restrains the devil from returning to the valley.

Folklorists have studied the tale of the devil in Presidio. One has written that "perhaps the myth and the ritual derive from the Indians' fear of supernatural influence and their desire to appease that power, and also from the early Spanish missionaries' attempts to phrase the message of the church in terms the Indians could comprehend."

Despite the analyses of learned men and women, the shrine continues to serve as a significant place of worship for the faithful, the believers in the story. Citizens of Presidio and Ojinaga have walked the tortuous trail up to the cave in their bare feet, braving the steep climb and the sharp rocks to atone for their sins and pray for forgiveness.

The stone shrine at the top of the mountains stands today, and inside can be found the Holy Cross. Candles set in bottles and jars are placed throughout. The entrance to the cave of the devil has been dynamited shut.

Despite the ritual of *El Día de la Santa Cruz* and regardless of the fact that the entrance to the cave has been sealed, Presidio and Ojinaga are still haunted by the devil, according to many. He continues to return to the area once known as La Junta to torment and mock those who live there. One resident reported that a group observed a jackrabbit dancing on its hind legs much as the devil did. When the rabbit was approached, it disappeared into thin air.

Others have claimed that during a Holy Cross Day celebration, the devil appeared in the form of a hunchbacked dwarf and was observed by dozens. While the priest chanted and blessed the crops, the dwarf led women into deep mud puddles, pushed men and boys into the river, and caused dogs to howl.

To a large percentage of the citizens of Presidio and Ojinaga, the hauntings of the devil are a far cry from myths and lore. To them, the devil is real and remains nearby.

CHAPTER 13

La Llorona

The terrorizing of the border area of Texas around the town of Presidio by a specter, believed by many to be the devil as described in the previous chapter, is not the only haunting associated with the Rio Grande. One ghostlike figure that has appeared to and frightened many is the apparition known as *La Llorona*, also known as the "wailing ghost woman" and "the weeping woman."

The origins of the La Llorona haunting are obscure and, like the aforementioned devil tale, may be centuries old. In the traditional version, La Llorona is a woman named Maria who is married to a wealthy landowner with whom she has two young children. (In some versions of the story, her name is given as Luisa.) Maria suspected her husband of infidelity. One evening, she followed him after he left the house and saw him with another woman. In a rage, Maria raced home, dragged her children to the Rio Grande, and drowned them. Though her objective was revenge against her husband, Maria immediately regretted her act. After dropping to her knees and saying a prayer, she cries out, *"Mis hijos! Mis hijos!"* ("My children! My children!") In her sorrow, Maria decides to join her offspring in the afterlife. She jumps into the river and drowns herself but, as the tale goes, is denied permission to be reunited with her children. Thereafter, her ghost walks the riverbank mourning her loss, weeping and wailing.

In a somewhat different version of this tale, Maria has two children born out of wedlock. In fear that the father will take them from her to be raised by his wife, she drowns them in the river. In this account, Maria does not commit suicide but rather spends the rest of her life and eternity walking the riverbank crying at the loss of her offspring.

In all of the tales of La Llorona, she is wearing a white dress and always walks the riverbank at night. Her cries, it is said, can be heard as much as a mile away. The story has its genesis in Mexican culture. Some folklorists argue that La Llorona is a story often told to children to frighten them into staying away from the river after dark, that bad things might happen to them.

The ghost of La Llorona, it is claimed, appears to people under different circumstances and throughout a wide geographic region. Though the tale of this specter is primarily associated with the Rio Grande that flows between Texas and Mexico, it has appeared elsewhere. At each region, her tale takes on a specificity pertinent to the local culture and geography. Folklorist Elton Miles claims that the story may have originated with the Aztecs. Miles writes that it is the story of a goddess dressed in white and carrying on her shoulders a cradle that . . . contained a child. She abandoned the cradle among a group of Aztec women, who found in it an arrow point shaped like a sacrificial knife. Afterward, the goddess would wander at night shrieking and weeping . . . and then disappear into the water of lakes or rivers.

One writer, Benjamin Radford, cites a similar tale from fifteenth-century Germany. Regardless of the origin of the tale, it is believed La Llorona's influence is felt as far south as Mexico City, as well as throughout the American Southwest. She has been portrayed in artwork and in theatrical productions, and a number of films have been produced purporting to tell her story.

When the desert of the Big Bend country of Texas receives ample rain and significant water flows in the draws and arroyos, it is said that the voice of La Llorona can be heard wailing "Mis hijos! Mis hijos!" Many claimed to have seen her over the years during such rains and stated that she is always "dressed in white, flowing garments." It has been said by some that to look into the face of La Llorona "is to see the face of your own death."

La Llorona's hauntings are not limited to the Rio Grande region of Texas. In Big Spring, La Llorona is described as a widow with two children living in poverty. For reasons unspecified, she drowns her children in Sulphur Draw, which flows with water from the spring after which the town is named. The act eventually drove the widow mad, and she could thereafter be seen and heard walking the banks of the draw, wailing. When she died, the townsfolk, instead of seeing to her burial, threw her body into the draw, just as she had done to her offspring. Every night, it is said, La Llorona can be heard crying for her babies.

There is yet another version of the La Llorona haunting, this one from El Paso. In this case, the woman, who has an illegitimate baby, is a thief. She lived in Juárez, Mexico, just across the river from El Paso. At night, she would cross the border to the Texas side of the river, break into houses, and steal whatever was of value. One night she broke into the home of a wealthy resident. No one was at home at the time, so she casually walked from room to room until she encountered a "large leather case inlaid with silver . . . crammed with gold money." She grabbed the case and ran.

Before she was able to vacate the property, the homeowner arrived and spotted her. He immediately alerted the police, and the pursuit was on. Believing she had been identified, the woman returned to her own house in Juarez, retrieved her baby, and hid in the brush along the Rio Grande. Her plan was to cross the river in the dark and escape back into El Paso.

Convinced she had eluded the police, the woman waded the river to the Texas side, the heavy leather satchel in one arm, her baby in the other. The river was only three feet deep, but the current was strong and, fearing she might slip under, she struggled to maintain her balance. Her baby, sensing the mother's terror, began to cry. Afraid that the pursuers might hear the child, she dunked the baby under the water and held it until it was dead. Moments later, the tiny body floated away with the current.

The woman made it safely to the riverbank on the Texas side. With the satchel full of money, she found herself to be a wealthy woman. It was said she lived "a long and frivolous life" in El Paso. When she died, those who knew her stated that she had never repented the murder of her child and was condemned to wander at night up and down the bank of the Rio Grande, weeping.

In the Texas towns of Fort Stockton and Alpine, the haunting of La Llorona has a slightly different twist. This version of the tale has been passed along in the oral tradition since at least the 1930s. In the accounts, the woman was married to a wealthy man, and they had two children. The woman abandoned her husband for another man, taking her children with her. When the husband found out, he flew into a rage and swore that he would burn her and the children alive for revenge. To spare the babies from such a fate, the woman, on a rainy night, carried them to a nearby stream and drowned them.

When the townsfolk learned of this deed, they seized the woman, dragged her to a cottonwood tree by the river, and hanged her. This done, they set her body afire and condemned her to struggle through the afterlife by wandering the stream where she drowned her babies, wailing all the while. On rainy nights in Alpine and Fort Stockton, it is said, her cries pierce the darkness. Those who hear her wailing express fear of going outside, fear of encountering La Llorona.

La Llorona, also referred to often as the Woman in White, is sometimes described as being the "guardian of hidden treasure." As recently as the 1970s, she has reportedly appeared to individuals in and near Presidio. She is always dressed in white and is sometimes described as glowing or being surrounded by flames. According to one man's account, the Woman in White appeared to him and beckoned for him to follow her, the implication being that she was to lead him to buried treasure. At first he fell in behind her but soon grew frightened and halted, refusing to continue any farther. At this, La Llorona simply disappeared.

In most of the tales of encounters with La Llorona, she is seen from a distance. Those few who have gotten close to her have related frightening experiences. On rare occasions, the otherworldly face of La Llorona has been gazed upon. One incident was related by Elton Miles in his book *More Tales of the Big Bend*. Two young men were walking together on a moonless night from their village in Mexico to a neighboring town across the river in Texas. They had planned to attend a dance that was being held there. A simple wooden bridge spanned the river. Following the dance, the youths, returning to their homes, crossed the bridge and made their way through a copse of trees.

Suddenly, one of the youths noticed a girl in the darkness, walking a short distance ahead of them and leaving the impression that she would like for them to catch up to her. Seeking to interact with this maiden who they had never seen before, the two hurried forward and moments later caught up with her. The three chatted for a few minutes, though the girl always remained several feet distant and in the shadows. In the darkness, the boys were unable to make out her features. Presently, one of them offered the girl a cigarette, which she accepted. When the second youth stepped forward, struck a match, and held it up to light her cigarette, the brief glow illuminated her face—a gruesome skull.

At the sight of the hideous apparition, the boys retreated several yards, on the verge of fleeing. The girl emitted a blood-curdling scream and, as they described later, "floated away toward the river."

For the most part, La Llorona is a specter witnessed almost entirely by Latin Americans. Over the centuries, she has become part and parcel of their culture. While many are eager to dismiss her as a mere folktale, even more are convinced she is real. Her story, in its many forms, has endured, even grown. Nearly every culture on earth possesses tales of and beliefs in ghosts, in hauntings, in monsters. Populations around the world are filled with tales of and alleged personal experiences with ghosts, poltergeists, vampires, werewolves, bigfoot, lake and sea monsters, and more. Many consider these tales and nothing more. Unlike the aforementioned monsters and ghosts, however, La Llorona is associated with a single ethnic group—Latin Americans—and has been experienced not only along the Rio Grande, where she seems to be the most prominent, but also deep into Mexico and throughout much of southern New Mexico.

The ethnic Mexican residents of the American Southwest as well as the country of Mexico insist that La Llorona is different from other specters. Many of them have had personal experiences with this ghost. They claim that there is no doubt she is real.

CHAPTER 14

The Ghost of the Rio Frio

In Texas, there is another strange tale of a ghostly female figure, this one sometimes seen walking along the banks of the Rio Frio in Real County, seventy miles due west of downtown San Antonio. She appears at first as a shapeless tendril of fog or mist on the bank of the river even though no other fog or mist can be seen. The mist slowly materializes into the form of a woman. This odd apparition has been seen for more than a century by hundreds of witnesses, and her story has become a prominent element of the culture in this part of Texas. Like La Llorona, this figure is always seen dressed in a long white flowing gown. Unlike her, the Ghost of the Rio Frio does not wail or cry; she has never been heard to utter a sound. It is, according to the tale, the ghost of a woman who was killed by a man who wished to possess her but had his intentions rebuked.

Rio Frio is an unincorporated community in South Texas adjacent to Highway 83 and supports a population of fifty. Fifteen miles downstream is Concan, another small community. The primary economic activity in the region is ranching as well as recreational activities associated with Rio Frio, including canoeing, kayaking, tubing, and fishing. The town was named after the river. A short distance upstream from Concan an incident occurred sometime during the mid-twentieth century that spawned one of the most famous hauntings in this fringe of the Texas Hill Country, a haunting that continues to this day.

The Rio Frio is a cool, clear-water stream that has its origin in springs in the northern part of Real County. (*Real* is the Spanish word for royal). The river flows from north to south until it reaches the southern part of Uvalde County, at which point it veers southeastward and miles later confluences with the Nueces River. The river has become a popular destination for canoeists and kayakers as well as fishermen, and as the throngs of recreationists have increased over the years, so have the sightings of the ghost dubbed the White Lady of the Rio Frio. During the short time that the White Lady is visible, some claim they can make out her face and describe her as beautiful. Then, moments later, she disappears.

This tale has its genesis in an actual event that took place during the early 1900s. Two sisters—Maria and Elena Juárez—lived with their family along the banks of the Rio Frio near the town of Concan and were known to be the prettiest girls in the area. Elena, the older of the two, married a man named Gregorio and had two children. Maria helped care for the children and dreamed of the day when she would be married and have babies of her own.

As Maria grew into her late teens, Gregorio became aware of her stunning beauty and found ways to spend more time with her when Elena was not around. Maria was oblivious to Gregorio's advances and at the same time was growing fond of a young man named Anselmo Tobar, who worked as a cowhand on a nearby ranch. Tobar was not immune to Maria's glances, and he soon began to court her. In time, the two spoke of marriage and began to make plans.

Gregorio was troubled, frustrated by Maria's infatuation with the young cowhand, and, in spite of the fact that he was married to her sister, despaired of losing her. One afternoon, Gregorio found Maria alone in the family garden, invited her to sit beside him on a bench, and confessed his love for her. Shocked at this revelation, Maria pulled away and informed Gregorio that she was in love with Anselmo and that they were to be married.

At this, Gregorio grew angry and began cursing, raging, and threatening. Frightened, Maria ran to her home and locked the door. That evening, as she and Anselmo had previously planned, the cowhand would pay her a visit. After the sun had gone down, Maria heard a noise outside. Believing it was Anselmo, she opened the door and ran into the darkness to greet him. Instead, she was surprised by the presence of Gregorio. Once again, he confessed his love for the young girl and promised her he would leave his wife, her sister, so that they could be married.

Calmly, Maria explained again her love for Anselmo. She told Gregorio that he needed to consider his wife's feelings and needs. She told him that it would be impossible for her to run off with her sister's husband.

Gregorio again flew into a rage. He begged and threatened Maria, but she held fast to her promise to Anselmo. Apparently prepared for such a rejection but unwilling to accept it, Gregorio pulled a revolver from his sash. As Maria backed away, he pointed the weapon and shot her in the heart, killing her instantly. As Gregorio stared at the dead body of the woman for whom he had professed love, townspeople who had heard the shot came running out of their houses. Fearing he would be identified, Gregorio ran to a nearby barn and hid beneath a stack of hay inside.

Within minutes, a crowd had gathered around Maria's body. Not a single citizen could imagine who would commit such a foul deed. With lanterns, several men ranged out to search the area for a suspect but had no luck. The following morning, more men arrived, bringing hunting dogs and guns. While the women of Concan prepared the beautiful Maria for burial, the men urged the dogs to pick up the scent of the culprit.

Confused, the dogs did little more than mill around the area where the body of Maria had lain. Presently, one of them set up a howl and raced over to the barn. It was immediately followed by the other dogs, all of them standing at the closed door of the barn and barking excitedly. One of the men opened the door, and the dogs ran inside toward a pile of hay stacked in a far corner. Standing before the hay, the dogs pointed and barked, more loudly this time. Guns were trained on the haystack. One man shouted an order for whomever was inside to come out with hands raised.

A portion of the haystack was pushed aside, and out stepped a lone man, hands raised high in surrender to the posse. In the dark shadows of the barn, the face of the man could not be seen clearly. When he was commanded to step forward, all in the crowd were surprised to see it was Gregorio. With rifles pointed at him, he tearfully confessed to killing Maria and once again swore his love for her.

Gregorio was placed under arrest to await trial. While he sat in his cell, plans for Maria's funeral proceeded. Her casket was adorned with flowers, and she was carried to the cemetery at the town of Rio Frio. For reasons unclear, her grave was not marked. She went to her final resting place, according to the citizens of the area, with her soul unfulfilled, her love for Anselmo not permitted to follow its natural course.

The court met only a few days after Maria's funeral. The trial was swift, and Gregorio was found guilty. One account of this tale claims that Gregorio was hung the next day. Another says he spent the rest of his life in prison.

The soul of Maria, they say, found no rest. It is claimed that her spirit roams the low canyon of the Rio Frio in the area between Rio Frio and Concan and that her aim is to comfort children in need. It has been said that the White Lady of the Rio Frio has occasionally been seen perched at the end of the bed of a sick child as if watching over it, guarding it from harm. It is said that adults, on seeing the ghost of the White Lady, feel fear and trepidation. Children, on the other hand, regard her as a kind and protecting spirit and do not fear her at all. Time and again, children have been known to ask their parents about the identity of the nice lady dressed in white who sat at the foot of their bed while they were sick.

CHAPTER 15

The Shelby County Hanging Tree

The following tale is unique among Texas hauntings in that one significant aspect of it was witnessed by dozens of people at the same time, believers and nonbelievers alike. The incident, though it occurred years ago, is still talked about today.

Center is an East Texas town. The seat of Shelby County is located seventeen miles west of the Louisiana border and boasts a population of 5,200 citizens. During the 1920s, Center was often in the national news for the lynching of African Americans. Blacks accused of crimes, real and imagined, were seized and hanged by mobs from a large oak tree located in front of the courthouse on the town square. The tree, known throughout the area as the "hanging oak," was cut down in 1990. Before it succumbed to chain saws, however, it left a frightening haunted message for the area citizens.

Though specific aspects of the genesis of this story are a bit sketchy, it is known that sometime during the 1920s, a Center, Texas, citizen by the name of John T. Wheeler was killed. Two of the town's residents out for a walk came upon the unfortunate Mr. Wheeler only moments after he was murdered and saw Moses Burke standing over him. Mr. Wheeler was white; Mr. Burke was black. In one hand, Burke held a piece of wood. To this day it is not known whether Burke killed Wheeler or if he merely came upon him moments after his death. Both men, it was subsequently learned, had been drinking to the point of drunkenness, though not necessarily together.

Sheriff Charlie B. Christian and City Marshall Bryan McCallum were summoned. Burke was immediately arrested and taken to the city jail, where he was held without bond. The county coroner, Dr. Tommy Hurst, determined that Wheeler met his death from a "blow to the head with a blunt object."

The 1920s was not a good time for black men in Shelby County, particularly ones accused of a crime. The region had a reputation for lynching blacks for the slightest of provocations and sometimes for no provocation at all. Within minutes following the discovery of the dead Mr. Wheeler, word spread throughout the town of Center, and soon an angry mob gathered, demanding that Burke be turned over to them. When Sheriff Christian refused to do so, the throng of perhaps two dozen men stormed the jail and pulled Burke from his cell. He was literally dragged, kicking and screaming, to the "hanging oak." Burke's hands were tied behind his back with bailing twine. A rope was obtained, a noose fashioned and secured over the head of Burke.

Sheriff Christian and Marshall McCallum, it was written, tried to prevent the lynching, but as they were outmanned and outarmed, they withdrew. Within minutes, Burke was swinging from the end of the rope two feet off the ground. He didn't die easily. Apparently, it took several minutes for the life to be choked out of Burke. All the while, his agonizing screams could be heard as much as a mile away—his cries for help, his protestations of innocence, a booming and disturbing sound that some citizens claimed they heard echoing and resounding for years.

After the mob departed, Christian and McCallum cut Burke down, carried him to the jail, and placed his body in one of the cells. The next day, the town undertaker took him to the funeral home and prepared him for burial. Burke was laid to rest two days later, one day following the funeral of John T. Wheeler. According to the citizens of Center, however, Burke did not rest quietly in his grave, for throughout the ensuing years, the night was occasionally rent with horrible screams that lasted as long as an hour, screams that seemed to issue from beneath his headstone. Those who heard the shrieks and cries identified them as the same as those that came from Moses Burke as he was swinging from the hanging tree during the moments before he perished.

According to the town's history, the hanging tree died a few months following the execution of Moses Burke, but no attempt was made to cut it down. And then, one year later, the tree miraculously came back to life, sprouting new limbs flush with green leaves. Over the years, there was talk of cutting the tree down, of ridding the town of an embarrassing and regrettable past, but despite the discussions, the tree remained.

As the years rolled on, reports of the ghostly screams of Moses Burke continued. Not only did the screams come from his grave but also, according to some, seemed to emanate from the hanging tree itself. There were those in town who insisted that the ghost of Moses Burke lived in the tree. Once, during the 1950s, an attempt was made to remove the tree from the square, but at the first strike of the ax, wails and moans appeared to come out of it, sounds that suggested someone was being tortured. Or hung. Those who would have cut down the tree threw down their tools and fled.

Several years later in 1969, another attempt was made to remove the hanging tree, but the results were the same. (One account gives the year as 1970.) James L. Choron, a reporter for the Center weekly newspaper, *The Champion,* was sent to the square to cover the event and take photographs. (Today, the newspaper is called *The Light and Champion.*)

On arriving, Choron took photos of the tree as the workers started up their chainsaws and prepared to go to work. Moments later, the air was filled with the sound of sputtering gasoline motors and spinning chains as they bit into the hard wood of the old tree. Suddenly, according to Choron's own article:

The otherwise still summer air was pierced by the most horrifying, blood-curdling scream that can possibly be imagined. It seemed to originate deep within the old oak, but was everywhere at once. It echoed off of the walls of the buildings lining the town square and literally beat its way into the consciousness of everyone present. Everyone on the square heard it. There was no mistake. I tried to get focused and get another photo of the tree. No luck. I was too busy to keep from being trampled by the departing work crew, who completely abandoned their chainsaws.

According to those at the scene, the cries that pierced the air sounded as if they were coming out of the tree itself. The crowd that had gathered was estimated to number close to thirty, and it was said that half of them fled in terror while the rest remained rooted to their position, stunned into shock and disbelief.

In 1990, a decision was made once and for all to remove the hanging tree. A work crew bearing chainsaws and other specific gear had arrived at the scene and prepared to carry out its assignment. During the removal process, some few observers claimed to have heard screams. Others insisted they were hearing the whine of the chainsaws and that the well-known cries of Moses Burke were absent.

There has been no definitive conclusion as to what has become of the ghost of Moses Burke. Most Centerites seem reluctant to talk about it but have expressed some conviction that, with the cutting down of the hanging tree, the haunting is over. Others, however, claim that on some nights they can still hear the screams.

CHAPTER 16

Huntsville's Haunted Cemetery

For centuries, cemeteries have been perceived as haunted places by a wide variety of cultures, a belief that holds true today throughout the world. There is a certain energy at such places, according to some, that is conducive to the support of ghosts and spirits. Across the United States, hundreds if not thousands of cemeteries are believed to be haunted, and stories of ghostly appearances have been related time and again.

Skeptics of such things tell us that creepy, unexplainable experiences related to cemeteries are little more than the by-product of imagination and fear. Most of them, it is said, can be easily dismissed. In many if not most cases, this is likely true, but there remain some accounts that are not so easy to reject. One cemetery that has the skeptics scratching their heads is located in Huntsville, Texas. It is called the Martha Chapel Cemetery, and the odd events that have occurred at this location have been going on for decades and have been witnessed by hundreds. A selection of strange hauntings associated with the Martha Chapel Cemetery are presented below.

Two men, longtime friends, had driven to the Martha Chapel Cemetery one afternoon to walk among the headstones, when they witnessed a bizarre sight. At one gravesite, an entire arm was protruding from the ground. The arm was described as "somewhat desiccated" and clothed in a rotted garment. On closer inspection, the two men stared in horror as they watched the arm moving, the hand seemingly searching for something on the sward. Despite the cautions expressed by his friend, one of the men, curious about what he was witnessing, advanced toward the grave. He leaned forward to get a better view of what he was seeing then reached out and grasped the hand. With an extremely strong grip, the hand and arm began pulling the man downward toward the grave.

The man, screaming in fright, fought hard against the pull, begging for help from his friend but receiving none. With a final jerk, he broke free of the grasping hand and turned to face his friend. The friend, rigid in his terror, simply stood unmoving, eyes wide in fright. Standing a few feet behind the friend, however, was a newcomer, his head glancing downward as though he were looking at the ground, his face obscured. The man who had been grasped by the hand stepped away from the grave and, passing his friend, advanced toward the stranger to ask him what he wanted. When the stranger looked up and the man saw his face, he was shocked to see that he looked exactly like his friend. When he turned around, his friend who had accompanied him to the cemetery, was gone.

The man, clearly confused and unnerved, ran from the gravesite toward his car. On arriving, he noted that the vehicle was covered in handprints in the dust on the surface. As he climbed into the car to start the engine, he noticed his friend sitting in the back seat. The friend was dead.

The strange appearance of handprints on vehicles parked at the cemetery occurred often. Over one hundred reports of such have been recorded over the years, and to date no explanation has been provided.

The bladed gravel lane that leads to the Martha Chapel Cemetery is officially named Bowden Road. To locals, however, it has another name, one more commonly used. It is called Demon's Road. Those who have walked or driven down Demon's Road over the years have reported odd encounters. According to writer Dana Goolsby, locals warn those who walk the path to visit the graveyard to be wary of spirits that may appear to them or that may follow them.

There have also been reports of strange red lights seen along Demon's Road, their origins unexplained. Those who claim to have seen the lights state that the number of glowing orbs always corresponds to the number of people walking or traveling in a vehicle. Sometimes during the appearance of the lights and without warning, handprints will materialize on the surfaces of the vehicle.

During late spring 2010, a group of friends and acquaintances were visiting the Martha Chapel Cemetery. It was evening, and a husband and wife spotted a lone man they had never seen before wandering slowly among the graves. He was dressed in a manner suggestive of the styles of sixty years earlier. Other than noticing his clothes, they paid little attention to him. A week later, the woman was in her bathroom preparing to enter the shower when she turned and saw the same man wearing the same period clothes standing in her bedroom. The woman screamed, and by the time she covered herself in a towel, the man had disappeared.

It gets stranger. Several people have alleged that while visiting the cemetery or walking along the lane, they have witnessed a "young child with glowing eyes riding a tricycle. The apparition will remain visible for a few seconds and then disappear. Others have reported seeing what they have described as a "strange, faceless, threatening creature" that appears out of nowhere. In every instance, those who claimed to have seen these specters insist that none of them ever indicated any desire to harm. Though they appeared threatening, frightening, they simply vanished or faded away.

The bizarre happenings associated with the Martha Chapel Cemetery have captured the attention of researchers and ghost hunters over the years, many of them arriving at the scene of the events as skeptics. By the time their investigations have concluded, they have become believers, but no logical explanations for the sightings and experiences have come forward.

THE REST

Chapter 17

The Mystery of the Iberian Tablet

Not all of the lost treasures associated with Texas are related to gold and silver ingots and coins. Paleontologists tell us that the Lone Star State is rich in fossils: reptilian, mammalian, and avian. In fact, the remains of the largest flying reptile ever found in the world was excavated in the Big Bend region of Texas, not far from the Mexican border. It was a pterosaur, a birdlike serpent larger than some fighter jets and with a wingspan of close to forty feet.

The Big Bend area has also been the setting for one of the strangest mysteries to face archeologists and historians, one that has nothing to do with precious metals or rare fossils. It has to do with man, but it is not related to a lost or cached treasure from a train robbery or mine. It is a clay tablet that provides stunning evidence that the Big Bend area of Texas was once visited by members of a lost civilization seventeen centuries before Indians occupied the region and perhaps as many as two thousand years prior to Christopher Columbus's historic voyage. When translated, the odd writing on the tablet was revealed to be a prayer. The tablet had been secreted in a small crevice, where it had lain for centuries. It was found by accident, retrieved, and turned over to the National Park Service. What happened to it after that represents yet another mystery associated with this remarkable find.

This saga begins during the Christmas holidays of 1961. Donald and Reva Uzzel of San Marcos, Texas, were joined by Donald's mother, Bernice, and her husband, Charles Nickles, who arrived from Alaska. Together, the group decided to travel to Big Bend National Park and spend a few days relaxing in the relative warmth of the Chihuahuan Desert environment. The park is located at the southern tip of Brewster County where the course of the Rio Grande shifts from flowing southeast to the northeast. The park encompasses 801,163 acres. It is a fascinating geologic area replete with faults and volcanic rock, all dominated by the majestic Chisos Mountains.

The four visitors checked into rooms at the lodge located in the Chisos Basin. The next morning following breakfast, they drove out to view the marvelous scenery found within the boundaries of the park. Their tour was filled with amazing desert scenery, and their route took them to Boquillas Canyon, where they intended to leave the car and hike. Little did they know they were about to make what some scholars consider to be one of the most amazing and important historical and archeological discoveries of our time.

Donald was driving eastward on a gravel road toward the canyon. At one point, he turned onto a side road that looked promising, followed its winding course, and finally arrived at the long-abandoned settlement of Hot Springs near the eastern boundary of the park and a short walk from the Rio Grande. The four took their time exploring around the old rock trading post and cabins. Not far from the post was the confluence of Tornillo Creek and the Rio Grande. The creek bed had only the merest trickle of water running through it in the shallow canyon in which it was located, and the two women suggested they walk upstream and look for some interesting rocks. Charles agreed to accompany them, but Donald said he was going to sit in the car and listen to the radio.

After the three disappeared around a bend up the creek, Donald grew restless and climbed out of the car. At first he intended to join the others, but after reaching the creek, he contented himself with examining a steep, nearly vertical rock face with prominent sedimentary layers. He decided to try to climb it. Years later when interviewed, Donald stated that he had this sudden feeling that he "needed" to climb the ledge. It was odd, he said, because he had never cared about climbing anything before in his life. As he sought hand- and footholds in the jutting layers of sedimentary rock, he gradually eased himself several feet up the steep incline. A moment after he began his ascent, the others could be heard coming back down the canyon.

Bernice, on spotting her son on the outcrop high above the stream bed, called for him to climb down, but Donald continued making his way upward, one handhold and one foothold at a time. According to another interview with Donald, he was standing on a narrow ledge that barely accommodated his feet when his fingers slipped into an opening in the rock just above. Concerned about the possibility of a rattlesnake lurking in the crevice, he quickly withdrew his hand. A moment later, however, he cautiously pulled himself up, peered into the dark hole, and "could see pieces of something stacked in there." He called down to the others, now waiting below, that he had found something.

Donald Uzzel described the crevice as L-shaped. The opening was four inches wide, nine inches high, and nineteen inches deep. At the end of this small chamber, the narrow passageway made a sharp turn to the left, paralleling the creek. It was twenty-two inches in length. The floor, ceiling, and walls were smooth. The "pieces of something" Donald saw were stacked in the portion of the hole in which his hand rested.

Donald withdrew one of the pieces and examined it. He found it very curious. Donald's mother took a position on a ledge just below him, his wife climbed to a point below her, and Charles found a perch near her. One by one, Donald withdrew the tiny pieces and passed them down. When Charles received one, he descended the short distance to a flat area below and laid it down carefully. Altogether, there were eleven pieces in a variety of shapes and sizes. They appeared to be made from clay and had the size and texture of tiles.

When the family was back on solid ground, they examined the pieces and were surprised to find that they fit together like a puzzle. By the time they had assembled it, it was twenty-one inches long and fourteen inches wide. On each piece were scratched what appeared to be letters of an alphabet none of them were familiar with. Charles retrieved his camera and shot several photographs of the odd tablet-like arrangement. Little did he know that these photos would soon be regarded as the only evidence of the curious discovery that would eventually generate intense interest among many archeologists and others interested in pre-Columbian settlement in America.

Donald described the pieces as being tan or brown. They were slick and shiny on the surface that held the writing and rough on the underside. The edges, he said, suggested it was once a larger tablet and that it had been broken apart, presumably to fit it into the small hole.

Donald returned to the car and found a small cardboard box into which he placed the artifacts. On entering the national park the previous day, he remembered seeing a sign stating that any artifacts found belonged to the US government. Believing their find to possess some historical or archeological importance, they decided to deliver it in person to ranger headquarters.

The first ranger they encountered at the visitors' center was David Evan, who was manning the counter and responding to tourists' questions. His badge identified him as the park's naturalist. On being presented with the cardboard box filled with the strange pieces of clay, accompanied by an explanation of where they were found, he responded skeptically. Donald had the feeling that Evan thought a joke was being played on him and acted like he wanted nothing to do with the artifacts. He tried to return them, but when Donald insisted, Evan took them and placed them under the counter.

Before leaving, the conscientious Donald gave Evan the names and addresses of all of the members of the party. As he drove away from the headquarters, Donald was confident that the National Park Service would do all they could to study and protect the artifacts. The four spent another day in the area and then returned to San Marcos. Several months later, Donald received a letter from Evan, who claimed "a man had inspected the tablet and could not make heads or tails of it."

Several months after that, Bernice and Charles Nickles encountered the writings of a man named Lewis R. Church. Church supported the growing belief, based on a wealth of evidence, of pre-Columbian European visitation to America. They wrote a letter to Church and included copies of the photos of the tablet taken by Donald Uzzel. On receiving the letter, Church contacted a Dr. Phillips, a Brigham Young University classical language scholar. After studying the tablet photographs, both men concluded that several of the characters resembled letters of an ancient Greek alphabet. As to how such a thing could have been found in a low dry canyon in a remote part of Texas, they offered no explanation.

Bernice and Charles Nickels moved back to Texas in 1964. They maintained an interest in the strange Big Bend tablet and continued to seek answers relative to its origin as well as a translation of the curious lettering. They sought advice from experts but received no positive responses. In 1969, they came across an article in a pulp magazine called *True West* that caught their interest. Bernice and Jack McGee wrote about pre-Columbian Scandinavian tombstones and runestones discovered in Oklahoma. In the article, the McGees invited readers to correspond with them about any strange inscriptions they might have stumbled onto. The Nickleses sent copies of the Big Bend tablet photos to the McGees, and the two writers spent years trying to interpret the letters.

While the McGees were studying the markings on the tablet, more and more information was coming to the fore relative to the accumulating evidence of pre-Columbian visitation to North America from across the seas. This evidence, overwhelming and difficult to deny, suggested that this continent had been visited by Europeans, North Africans, Asians, and Middle Easterners long before the time of Christ. The pre-Columbian Scandinavian voyages of Leif Erikson to the North American continent have long been substantiated, and additional evidence suggests he arrived on the heels of other Norsemen. Further, inscriptions on rocks and metal found throughout parts of the American Southwest are clearly of Phoenician and Jewish origin.

The McGees pursued their research on the tablet with vigor. They wanted to see the original pieces found by Uzzel and contacted officials at Big Bend National Park. Their inquiry was forwarded to the present chief naturalist, Roland Wauer. Time passed, and Wauer wrote to the McGees telling them he had contacted David Evan, the ranger who accepted the pieces of tablet from Uzzel on behalf of the government. At the time, Evan was stationed at a national monument in Nevada. He said he recalled Uzzel handing him a box containing some unidentifiable pieces of clay. Evan described each of them as a "cake of sun-dried mud that could have been peeled from the bottom" of any mud-soaked creek. He said the fragments were not weathered, and he judged them to have been made recently, probably by Uzzel himself.

According to Evan, the pieces of tablet

lay in my office in the Maintenance Building for many weeks. I showed it to any and all who might be able to shed some light on it. Everyone agreed it had no historical significance. It disintegrated from handling, and the move down to the new Administration Building turned it into a pile of dust . . . no one who saw it believed it had any antiquity. The consensus was that a Mexican goatherd had sat and doodled in the mud with a stick.

It is difficult to believe that the pieces of hard, shiny clay tiles described by Uzzel could have disintegrated into dust, as Evan stated, in such a short time. Some have conjectured that it is more likely that Evan either lost the pieces or threw them away. Others have suggested that Evan lied and passed the pieces of tablet to someone else. Research into Evan's comments, along with pertinent developments that have taken place over subsequent years, have yielded enough information to conclude that the park ranger was less than truthful. Still others have advanced the notion that the artifacts were stored and perhaps forgotten at some unknown location on national park property, where they might remain today.

The McGees, disappointed but not discouraged, decided to travel to Big Bend National Park and search for the tablet's original hiding place as described by Uzzel. Before doing so, they sent copies of the inscriptions to Dr. Cyclone Covey, a professor of ancient history at Wake Forest University in North Carolina. Following his analysis, Covey concluded that the writing "consisted of primitive Greek characters mixed with those of another alphabet" neither he nor anyone else could identify.

Covey passed along an interesting observation to the McGees in his correspondence. Most researchers at the time, he said, assumed that pre-Columbian visitors to this continent had floated up the Mississippi River and into its tributaries such as the Arkansas and Missouri Rivers. He suggested that it might be possible that whoever left the Big Bend tablet may have come *down* the Rio Grande from a source upstream. Would it have been possible, asked the historian, that groups could have crossed the Pacific Ocean, trekked across the western part of the North American continent, and come down rivers such as the Arkansas, Missouri, and Rio Grande? Covey pointed out that an ancient tombstone with Greek markings on it had been found near Cripple Creek, Colorado, not far from the Rio Grande. He also noted that near Albuquerque, close to the confluence of the Rio Grande and the Puerco River, an inscription was found on a cave wall that was identified as ancient Phoenician or Jewish, two languages that were very similar. Translated, the writings turned out to be the Ten Commandments. Not far from Tucson, Arizona, the remains of a centuries-old settlement has been uncovered, and among the artifacts found were some inscribed with Hebrew writing.

In December 1970, the McGees invited the Uzzels, now living in Bastrop, Texas, and the Nickleses, now living in Brenham, Texas, to meet in Big Bend to try to find the L-shaped crevice in which Donald found the pieces of tablet. They were joined by naturalist Wauer. Together, the group made their way to the rock face next to Tornillo Creek. After an hour of searching, Donald found it. It was higher than he remembered, some thirty feet above the creek bed, he said. The party searched other small openings in the ledge up and down the creek but located nothing of interest.

Examining the creek bed, one of the investigators found a type of mud called bentonite. It was described as "a reddish, mineral clay with iron content, formed by decomposed volcanic ash." They sent samples of the mud to Dr. Covey, who said that as it dried, "it became lighter in color," approximating the photograph of the tablet earlier provided by the Nickleses.

With the photographs and witnesses, the existence of the mysterious tablet was further confirmed. Even the kind of mud it might have been made from was identified. But what did the inscriptions on the strange artifact say?

In 1977, the McGees were apprised of the writings of Dr. Barry Fell. Fell authored a book entitled *America B.C.: Ancient Settlers in the New World*, which contained illustrations of pre-Columbian and pre-Christian epigraphs found in North America believed to have been made by Celts, Iberians, Libyans, and Norsemen, all visitors to the continent long before the voyage of Columbus. Fell was criticized by mainline archeologists who were devoted to the premise that early visitors and inhabitants of North America arrived via the Bering Strait land bridge. Over time, Fell was proven correct and the archeologists wrong. Through Dr. Covey, the McGees contacted Fell.

Fell, a linguist specializing in ancient languages, wrote that the message on the tablet was "written illiterately in Iberian language, using debased Homeric-Iberic script." Lines five and six, he added, were written "in Iberic, Lycian, and Lydian" and he determined somehow that it was done around 302 AD. Iberia is the ancient name for the Spanish peninsula. The Iberian alphabet, according to Fell, evolved from Phoenician. Lycia was a country located in Asia Minor on the Mediterranean Sea. The Lycians were conquered by Lydians, whose kingdom was on the Aegean Sea, thus mixing people and languages.

The Iberian Tablet

According to Elton Miles in *Stray Tales of the Big Bend,* the three cultural groups mentioned were subjects of the Roman Empire. All three belonged to cultures that possessed huge fleets of ships and advanced navigational skills, all quite capable of crossing the Atlantic Ocean in ships and arriving at the East Coast of North America.

The next obvious question is: How did this tablet containing Iberian, Lycian, and Lydian writing wind up in the Texas Big Bend? That remains a mystery that perplexes researchers to this day.

And what of the translation of the tablet? It appears to be a prayer:

Why this suffering?
Ah, what anguish!
A call to prayer—29 December
First winter month—Year 6
Heal us!
Heal us! Heal us!

The faithful by sorrow are beset;
O guide us, Mithras.
Show forth thy power and
The promise of aid as
Revealed by Ahura-
Mazda.
Amen

The first "Heal us!" in the first stanza is written in Iberic, the second in Lycian, the third in Lydian.

Author Miles concludes that "a party of ancients representing three languages were pleading to Mithras for mercy." During that time, Mithraism was a popular religion throughout the Roman Empire and rivaled Christianity, to which it shares a number of similarities. Ahura-Mazda was described as the one true god by Zoroaster, a prophet in the Zoroastrian religion. It may well be, according to Dr. Covey, that those who placed the tablet pieces in the tiny hole near Hot Springs in the Big Bend were Zoroastrians. The caching of the pieces of the tablet containing the prayer is not unlike the ritual involving prayer walls found in certain parts of the world in which people place a written supplication in a hole or crevice.

One question commonly asked by skeptics is: Could the tablet be a forgery or prank? There is always that possibility, but consider the following: Who could have written such a thing in three long dead languages known only to a very few specialized scholars? Who would know of the ancient religion invoked in the prayer save only a few? Why hide such a thing in a tiny hole some thirty feet above a creek bed where the likelihood of it ever being discovered was minimal? And to what end?

Some have suggested that Donald Uzzel himself made the tablet and concocted the story to bring some modicum of recognition to himself. Uzzel possessed a high school education and nothing more in the formal sense. During his lifetime, he worked as a sheriff's deputy, operated a television leasing company, and was employed by Dow Chemical in Freeport, Texas. These are hardly credentials for writing in ancient script. Other than having been mentioned in association with the discovery of the tablet pieces,

Uzzel received little to no recognition and profited not one dime from the experience.

The Nickleses possessed backgrounds similar to Uzzel and were clearly incapable of perpetuating such a hoax. Thus, it stretches credibility that any of these people had the knowledge and ability related to writing a translatable Mithran prayer in a language that was last used around 300 AD. Most extensively educated and trained language scholars cannot do it.

And how did the pieces of the tablet come to be placed in a difficult-to-reach rock crevice near the Rio Grande in what is now Texas? It has been conjectured that a party of explorers with Iberian connections had made their way into the region. No evidence has ever been found of any kind of settlement linked to them. Were they simply passing through the region on their way to somewhere else? We will likely never know.

And what of the original pieces of the tablet? Could the solid, irregular tiles, apparently made from clay and described as "hard," have simply disintegrated into dust as park naturalist David Evan claimed? It would seem unlikely. It would appear, on the surface, that Evan made up the story to cover the possibility that he may have either thrown the tiles away, placed them in some storage container and forgot them, or gave them away. Such things have happened. His claim that they disintegrated into dust while sitting on his windowsill is difficult to believe.

Since the discovery of the Big Bend tablet by Donald Uzzel, dozens of other objects and writings have been found on the North American continent that lend credence to the notion that it was visited by members of other civilizations long before Columbus ever entered adjacent seas. How and why these emissaries of a foreign land came to the Texas Big Bend remains a compelling and tantalizing mystery.

A private investigator specializing in historical mysteries has recently invested some time and energy tracking down information regarding the mysterious Iberian tablets found in the Big Bend region of Texas. He learned about them from his wife's ex-husband, who was related to Donald Uzzel. During his investigations, the detective learned that the tablets were neither lost nor "disintegrated," as described by national park ranger David Evan. Following his assignment at Big Bend National Park, Evan was transferred to a national monument in Nevada. From the available evidence, Evan took the pieces of the tablet with him. Why he decided to take possession of the artifact and then claim it had been destroyed is unknown and curious. Following Evan's death, his possessions, including the tablet pieces, became the property of his widow, who settled in Dallas, Texas. With her passing, all of her belongings were transferred to a daughter. The detective is convinced that the daughter still possesses the tablet, and at this writing he is in the process of attempting to locate her.

CHAPTER 18

The Aurora UFO Incident

Unidentified flying objects, as well as aliens from other planets, have become part and parcel of America's culture for well over the past half century. Belief in flying saucers and extra-terrestrials is widespread, and organizations have been established to facilitate research on the topic. Alleged evidence for such appears to be abundant but is largely inconclusive. Absolute proof of alien craft and beings remains nonexistent. Still, certain reported events alleging alien visitation have left much of the population in a state of wonder.

Fifty years before the famous 1947 Roswell incident, wherein an alleged spacecraft crashed in the New Mexico desert and reportedly yielded bodies of space creatures, a similar incident occurred in the small town of Aurora, Texas. It was witnessed by several. What was found was documented, but what actually happened remains a mystery.

Aurora is located just off US Highway 287, twenty-five miles northwest of Fort Worth. In 1897, the population was around 400. Today it is listed as 1,220. Around 6:00 a.m. on the morning of April 17, 1897, according to an article in the *Dallas Morning News* penned by reporter E. E. Haydon, a strange craft described as an "airship" sailed over the Aurora public square and continued northward toward the home and property of Judge J. S. Proctor. (Another account provides the date of April 19, 1897. Yet another

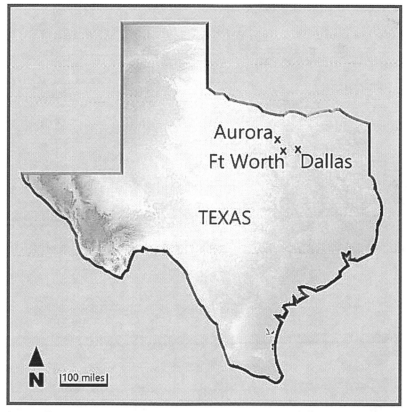

Aurora, Texas

gave Haydon's initials as S. E. rather than E. E.) Flying low to the ground, the "alien" craft struck the judge's windmill, toppling it and destroying the adjacent water tank. A moment later, the craft exploded, scattering debris across several acres.

The newspaper article stated that the "pilot of the ship is supposed to have been the only one aboard and, while his remains were badly disfigured, enough had been recovered to show that he was not an inhabitant of this world."

Haydon goes on to relate that US Army Signal Corps officer T. J. Weems provided the opinion that the pilot "was a native of the planet Mars," though how he would know or even suspect such a thing is not clear. Papers found on the pilot contained writing that was described as "unknown hieroglyphics" and could not be deciphered. The craft, according to those who examined it, was constructed of some unknown metal "resembling a mixture of aluminum and silver, and . . . weighed several tons." It could not be determined what powered the craft.

The badly burned body of the presumed pilot of the ship was carried to the Aurora Cemetery and buried "with Christian rites." Today, a marker at the entrance of the cemetery provides some history as to its origin along with the names of a few prominent citizens buried there. Near the end of the marker's information is found this sentence: "This site is also well-known because of a legend that a spaceship crashed nearby in 1897 and the pilot, killed in the crash, was buried here."

Much of the debris from the wreckage was gathered up and dumped into the well that was located beneath the windmill. A few of the pieces, it was learned, were buried with the "alien" in the cemetery. A few days later, military personnel visited Aurora and gathered up some of the remaining crash debris. They told residents they were going to analyze it, but nothing was ever heard from them.

In 1945, Aurora resident Brawley Oates purchased Judge Proctor's property and opened a gas station near the highway. Determined to use the old well as a water source, he cleaned out most of the metal fragments from the spacecraft that had been deposited there. Over time, Oates developed a severe and dramatic case of arthritis that he claimed resulted from drinking water that had been contaminated by the "alien" wreckage. In 1957, Oates sealed the well, covering it with a concrete slab over which he constructed a shed.

News of the Aurora incident did not travel far beyond the immediate area, and soon the matter was largely forgotten for over three-quarters of a century. In May 1973, however, a United Press International report revived the incident and described legal proceedings underway to exhume the body of the pilot of the craft.

A few days later, another UPI report quoted Mary Evans, a ninety-one-year-old resident of the town who recalled the crash. She had been fifteen at the time and "had all but forgotten the incident" until it was brought to the attention of the American public in the newspapers. She recalled that her parents had gone to the site of the crash but insisted that she remain at home. Evans recalled that the remains of "a small man" had been buried in the Aurora Cemetery.

Charlie Stephens, another Aurora resident who was ten at the time, recalled seeing the slow-moving airship trailing smoke as it headed toward the town. He wanted to go see the crash, but his father made him stay home and finish his chores. Later, his father, who went to see the wreckage, described it to him.

A short time later, an Associated Press report carried the information that a professor from North Texas State University had found some odd metal fragments near the Oates gas station located on the old Proctor property. The professor said one fragment was particularly intriguing because it consisted primarily of iron but exhibited no magnetic properties whatsoever and that it was "shiny and malleable instead of dull and brittle like iron."

The Aurora Cemetery Association blocked all attempts to excavate the grounds in search of the alleged alien remains. A tombstone had been placed over the site years earlier, but it had been stolen. Today, the actual location of the grave of the craft's pilot is not clear.

Over the years, unidentified pieces of metal have been found in the area of the old Proctor property, presumed by some to be debris from the craft. When word got out about the finds, according to some Aurora residents, military personnel appeared and confiscated the fragments.

There exists another side to this story. A few who have studied this event have contended the Aurora spaceship crash was a hoax. Barbara Brammer, a former mayor of Aurora, is one who questions the notion that an alien craft came down in the town. She stated that during the time of the alleged crash, the cotton crop, the major source of income for the town, had been devastated by a boll weevil infestation. A short time later, a fire on the west side of town destroyed several buildings and took a few lives. Not long after this, an epidemic of "spotted fever" struck the area, "nearly wiping out the remaining citizens and placing the town under quarantine." Finally, plans for a railroad stop in the town were changed and the tracks bypassed Aurora. The town, claims Brammer, was in danger of dying out. As a result, reporter Haydon, who Brammer described as a "bit of a jokester," wrote the spaceship crash article as a last-ditch attempt to keep Aurora alive, economically speaking.

In a 1979 *Time* magazine article, Aurora resident Etta Pegues supported Brammer's contention that Haydon fabricated the entire event in order to "bring interest to Aurora." Pegues claimed there was never even a windmill on Judge Proctor's property, a contention that was disputed by several of the town's old-timers.

During the early 2000s, an investigative team from MUFON (Mutual UFO Network) arrived at the cemetery with the goal of disinterring the body of the airship pilot to determine once and for all whether it was an alien. According to their report, they "uncovered a grave marker that appeared to show a flying saucer of some sort." Using a metal detector, they recorded strong readings from something immediately below the marker. The team requested permission to excavate the site and exhume the body and any pieces of metal but were denied.

A short time after the visit by the MUFON investigators, the marker disappeared, and a three-inch-diameter pipe was placed into the ground at the site for unknown reasons. A subsequent visit to the site by the team yielded no indication of metal in the grave. It was presumed that whatever had been buried there had been removed since their last visit. Who would have done such a thing remains unknown.

In 2008, Tim Oates, current owner of the property where the spacecraft crashed, allowed investigators to unseal the well and examine any debris they might find below. Water drawn from the well was tested and found to contain a high concentration of aluminum. No metal debris was found in the well, and Oates explained that a previous owner of the property had it all removed. The remains of the base of a windmill were found nearby, which further refuted the earlier statement by Etta Pegues that there never was such a structure on Judge Proctor's property.

The Aurora incident has been investigated by dozens of people, written about, featured numerous times on television, and even made into a movie.

On the other hand, what actually happened at Aurora in 1897 is not entirely clear. If it had been an obvious attempt at a hoax, the occasional appearance and involvement of military personnel would not have been warranted. Furthermore, the evasive responses and suspected tampering associated with the so-called alien grave generates suspicion.

What happened in Aurora in the early morning of April 17, 1897? To this day, no one seems to know for certain.

In recent years, an alternative explanation for the 1897 Aurora, Texas, incident has surfaced. Extant writings and explanations related to the event have caused investigators to arrive at a conclusion considerably different from the accepted legend. Here are the facts:

1. The airship was described as "cigar-shaped," flying low to the ground at a speed of "ten or twelve miles an hour and gradually settling toward the earth," according to reporter Haydon.
2. The airship was estimated to have weighed "several tons" and appeared to have been made from "a mixture of aluminum and silver."
3. The pilot was "badly disfigured" and enough of his remains had been "picked up to show that he was not an inhabitant of this world."
4. Papers were found on the body of the pilot that were written "in some unknown hieroglyphics and cannot be deciphered."
5. Mary Evans was told by her parents that the "remains of a small man" had been buried in the Aurora Cemetery.

The investigators have advanced the notion that the "unidentified flying object" was not a spaceship at all but rather a small Zeppelin. The Zeppelin was a rigid airship, cigar-shaped, a framework made of aluminum and copper, and contained rubberized cotton gasbags to provide lift. They were powered by one to several engines. The Zeppelin was patented in Germany in 1895 and came into use within months.

Is there a possibility that it could have been a Zeppelin that crashed on the Proctor farm in 1897? This option has been embraced by a handful of researchers. During this time, it is a fact that Germans had established secret military installations in Mexico. Germany had a keen interest in the political developments in Mexico and even contributed to the revolutionary cause. This was also a time of significant railroad construction in the United States, and the Germans monitored this progress. One way they accomplished this was to launch Zeppelins during the night and conduct aerial surveys throughout much of Texas. It was suggested that the sparse population and abundance of places to hide kept the Zeppelins from being spotted.

In the case of the Aurora incident, the airship, according to observers, was clearly experiencing some in-flight difficulties, causing it to descend from its observation altitude and crash onto the Proctor property, where it exploded, sending debris across a wide expanse of countryside.

The pilot of the airship was described as "not of this world" and "badly disfigured." Due to the explosion, there is little doubt that the pilot was burned, likely beyond recognition. It is also a fact that when a human body has burned, the tendons and ligaments contract, causing the corpse to shrink and shrivel, further adding to the disfigurement. Mary Evans recalled that she was told the remains of a "small man" had been buried in the cemetery. Note she used the word "man" not "creature" or "alien."

It was stated that "papers were found on the body containing unknown hieroglyphics." It seems odd that the body was burned to a state of disfigurement yet papers survived. What were described as hieroglyphics may have been German script or code.

To many, this alternative explanation of the Aurora UFO incident may seem just as bizarre as the one that claims a spaceship from Mars crashed in the small town, and the debate continues. Whatever the truth, the Aurora occurrence continues to remain a prominent Texas mystery.

CHAPTER 19

The Continuing Mystery of the Marfa Lights

On most nights of the year, south of a stretch of Texas State Highway 90 called Mitchell Flat and located ten miles east of the small town of Marfa, Presidio County, one can observe one of the most perplexing mysteries in North America. The puzzle involves strange lights, the origins of which are obscure, yet they have been observed for hundreds of years. Explanations for their existence are many and varied and, for the most part, inconclusive, but they continue to perplex those who claim expertise in such things.

The Marfa Lights have been described as balls of brilliance that appear to hover just above the desert floor. They are sometimes described as stationary, pulsing on and off with "intensity varying from dim to almost blinding brilliance." Other times, the lights dart to and fro across the desert flats, occasionally splitting and then merging. The colors of the lights vary. Yellow-orange is most often seen, but green, blue, and red have also been reported. During one spate of sightings in the 1960s, pink and pale yellow were the most often mentioned.

In recent years, a viewing area has been established on the south side of Highway 90 from which observers can watch the phenomena. As the lights bob and weave across the area, they blink and glow, sometimes vanishing only to reappear seconds or minutes later. Thus far, it has been impossible to determine how far from the road the lights conduct their nightly mystery dance. Estimates have ranged from a few yards to dozens of miles. Even more bizarre, some observers claim to see the lights while others standing nearby can't see them at all.

Marfa is not the only place where similar mysterious lights have appeared. There are three other locations: a remote area in northeastern Australia; the Hessdalen Valley in Norway; an isolated stretch of the Mekong River in Thailand. It is unclear what similarities, if any, are shared by the three sites, and the few who have researched the locations insist there are none.

The first recorded account of the Marfa Lights appeared in 1863. As he was driving cattle from one location to another one evening, a sixteen-year-old cowhand named Robert Reed Ellison spotted lights flickering in the distance. At first, he thought that they were the campfires of Apache Indians, who were known to frequent the region. With this in mind, Ellison proceeded with caution. When Reed mentioned his observation to others, he was informed that the strange lights had often been seen by many who lived and worked the cattle in this area. Like Reed, they initially suspected Indian campfires, but on investigation no evidence of such was ever found. After Reed's revelations, others who lived in the area came forward with their own stories of seeing the lights.

During World War II, pilots from Midland Army Airfield conducted flights over the Mitchell Flat area in an attempt to discern the source of the mystery lights. Following repeated attempts, they returned to the base with no explanation for the phenomena. On another occasion, a jeep containing two soldiers was sent out into Mitchell Flat to chase down and discern the source and identity of the lights. (Another report claims the jeep carried four men—two soldiers and two research scientists.) The men in the jeep carried a two-way radio in order to remain in contact with military headquarters.

One report stated that a short time after arriving close to one of the lights, the two-way radio went dead, communication ceased, and the men failed to return from the area. The following day, a search party went to the location and found the jeep, but there was no sign of its passengers. Oddly, a single military-issue wool sock was found nearby.

A second report stated that a military observer stationed approximately one mile away used his two-way radio to guide the men in the jeep toward the light. When he informed them they had reached it, that they were, in fact, right next to it, the jeep's passengers claimed they could see nothing. At that point, the radio went dead. The next morning, a search party was sent into Mitchell Flat to find the missing men. Following a two-hour search, the jeep's passengers were found. They had been thrown from the vehicle and had burned to death.

A third report claimed that when the occupants of the jeep did not report back, a rescue party went in search of them the following day. It found the jeep; it had burned so hot that the metal had melted. There was no sign of the scientists. Yet another version of this investigation claimed that the two scientists were later found but were in a state of shock from which they never recovered. They were both sent to sanitariums, where, according to this account, they remained for the rest of their lives.

It must be pointed out that, while the above versions have circulated throughout this part of the Southwest for more than half a century, legitimate verification has been difficult to come by. Some observers insist that these accounts point to the notion that there exists an element of evil associated with the Marfa Lights and that to encounter them is to court disaster, even death. Others, however, tell a different story. Mrs. W. T. Giddens related a remarkable tale of how the mysterious Marfa Lights saved the life of her father.

The elder Giddens was making his way home to Marfa from Mexico. He had crossed the Rio Grande and was headed north-northeast on foot. While in the area of Chinati Peak, twenty-five miles southwest of town, he got caught in a blizzard. As he was close to freezing to death, the lights came upon him. According to the father, the lights guided him to a small cave in the mountain range, and within that bit of shelter, he survived the night. One of the lights remained near him, he claimed, providing warmth.

Giddens was not the only person to claim he was saved by the lights. During the early part of the twentieth century, a cowhand was working in the area of the Chinati Mountains when he, like Giddens, was caught in a blizzard. Lost and disoriented, the cowhand despaired of surviving when a ghost light appeared. He spurred his horse in an attempt to get away from it, but it followed him. When he was finally convinced the light intended no harm, the cowhand halted his mount and turned to face it. The light moved off in a different direction, and the cowhand felt compelled to follow it. After several miles, the light suddenly disappeared, and the cowhand found himself a short distance from the town of Presidio, several miles to the south.

During the early 1950s, the movie *Giant* starring Rock Hudson, Elizabeth Taylor, and James Dean was made in and around the town of Marfa. Dean, it was told, had been fascinated by the Marfa Lights, and during the evenings when filming was halted, he would drive his costars out to the viewing area near Mitchell Flat so they could watch them. As it turned out, Dean was the only one who could see them.

The first published account of the Marfa Lights appeared in the July 1957 issue of *Coronet* magazine. Soon afterward, the curious from all over the United States arrived at Marfa to see the glowing orbs for themselves. More articles followed, more publicity generated, and today the lights are considered a natural wonder, one that continues to attract visitors to the area and that has thus far eluded explanation.

During the past half century, dozens, if not hundreds, of experts have arrived at Mitchell Flat with the sole purpose of researching and learning the source of the mystery lights. They have included geologists, physicists, astrophysicists, meteorologists, engineers, and others. One so-called expert was a man named Brian Andrew Dunning, who hosted a weekly podcast titled *Skeptoid*. In the past, Dunning has critically examined alleged scientific and paranormal mysteries including crop circles, mystery lights, and medical quackery, as well as creation legends. According to Dunning, the most logical explanation for the Marfa Lights was that they were a "mirage caused by sharp temperature gradients between the cold and warm layers of air." The truth is temperature differentials between layers of air of as much as 50 degrees Fahrenheit are common in this area of Texas. The problem with Dunning's explanation, however, is that the lights are often seen when no such differentials exist.

In 1988, an Englishman named Paul Devereux arrived in the area to investigate the lights. Devereux stated that he had investigated similar phenomena in the British Isles and insisted there was a correlation between the locations where sightings occurred and patterns of geologic faulting. He claimed that "prehistoric megalithic sites are sometimes located where mystery light sightings are still being reported today." Devereux referred to them as "earthlights." Whether Devereux's speculations have any relevance to the Marfa Lights has yet to be officially determined.

In May 2004, a group of physics students from the University of Texas at Austin arrived at Mitchell Flat and invested four nights in recording the lights they observed southwest of the viewing area. They brought with them video cameras, binoculars, traffic volume–monitoring equipment, and other scientific paraphernalia. They concluded that the frequency of lights viewed to the southwest correlated with the frequency of vehicle traffic on US Highway 67, which runs from Marfa south-southwest to the Mexican border. They also documented that the lights appeared in a straight line, one which corresponded to the route of US 67. In the end, the University of Texas group stated that "all lights observed over a four-night period southwest of the view park could be reliably attributed to automobile headlights traveling along US 67 between Marfa and Presidio, Texas."

It is a fact that traffic running along US 67 can be seen from the Highway 90 viewing area, and the conclusions arrived at by the scientists have some merit. However, their experiment does not explain the lights that are seen to the south and to the southeast of the viewing area, nor does it explain the variety of colors observed.

In May 2008, another group of scientists from Texas State University at San Marcos applied spectroscopy equipment to observe the Marfa Lights from the viewing station. They recorded lights on several occasions and provided the explanation that they came from either automobiles or small fires. This report left many familiar with the story of the lights unsatisfied. The lights had been seen for decades, if not centuries, prior to the construction of the highways. The notion of the source of the lights being "small fires" was absurd.

Another explanation offered over the years relates to the notion that the Marfa Lights are caused by gases such as phosphine and methane. Under certain conditions, these gases can ignite on contact with oxygen. The result is what has been described as a "glowing phenomenon," sometimes called "will-o'-the-wisp" and "*ignes fatui,"* or fool's fire. These have been observed principally in marshy areas where the decay of organic matter can generate pockets of phosphine and methane, hence the term *marsh gas*, which has been blamed for the appearance of mysterious lights at various places around the world. This explanation for the Marfa Lights falls apart as a result of the fact that there are no marshes within one hundred miles of Mitchell Flat. There are, however, significant reserves of oil, natural gas, and other petroleum hydrocarbons in this region, which can include methane in quantities capable of producing a similar effect.

James Bunnel, a retired aerospace engineer, is convinced that the Marfa Lights are the result of the igneous rock located under Mitchell Flat that "creates a piezoelectric charge." This is defined as electricity produced under pressure by solid matter such as minerals or crystals.

Bunnel's hypothesis is not shared by all. Karl Stephan, a Texas State University engineering professor is one such skeptic. Stephan states that Bunnel's theory is "all speculation at this point." In response to Stephan's skepticism, Bunnel came up with yet another theory. He postulated that "the lights may result from all the high-energy particles, or plasma, that rain down from the inner Van Allen Radiation Belt." Bunnel claims that "while most are absorbed into the planet, some . . . may be repelled by the layer of volcanic rock in the Mitchell Flat, which behaves like a magnetic shield. This hot, ionized plasma then shoots around, splitting and recombining and glowing like mad."

The explanations involving vehicle lights coming from US 67 has grown to become the most common one offered by skeptics. It must be pointed out, however, that US 67 did not exist when cowhand Robert Reed Ellison described the lights in 1863.

And then there is this: Marfa locals and some old-timers have whispered that there are two different kinds of Marfa Lights—the real ones and the phony ones viewed from the observation point near Mitchell Flat.

Kerr Mitchell lives at the southern end of Mitchell Flat, a geographic feature named for his family. Mitchell has seen the real Marfa Lights. He described one of them as a "massive, enormous white light." Another time he saw "five or six in a series" moving at a rapid speed. "What I saw," said Mitchell, "made me a believer." The phony lights, says Mitchell, are the ones seen from the viewing area on Highway 90. "It's good for tourists," he says.

The Marfa Lights have been observed for hundreds of years. The American Indians who live in the area have been aware of them for a long time and refer to them as the "spirits of the Chisos Apaches" and "departed relatives." Regardless of their explanations, it is a fact that, according to the oral tradition, Indians have observed these lights for hundreds of years, long before Anglo settlement in the area.

Over the decades, numerous explanations have been offered for the Marfa Lights, but thus far no one has arrived at a definitive conclusion. They continue to baffle, tantalize, and confound and remain a mystery.

CHAPTER 20

How Did Davy Crockett Die?

One of the most enduring images embraced by Americans is that of Alamo hero Davy Crockett, in particular the one portrayed by actor Fess Parker. In episode three of the 1955 Walt Disney television series, Crockett, having fired his weapon and with no time to reload, is last seen defending a wall and swinging his trusted long rifle against an attacking throng of Mexican soldiers. As the final scene fades and the theme music rises, Crockett is still battling, the implication being that the brave defender met his end while fighting to the last for an ideal—Texas's independence from Mexico.

In a variety of surveys taken over the years, Americans were asked about their perceptions of heroic figures. When asked how Davy Crockett perished, nearly everyone, likely influenced by the Disney film, replied that he died in defense of the Alamo, fighting to the very last. But is that the truth? As it turns out, as more and more research has been done on the Battle of the Alamo and Davy Crockett, strong and compelling evidence surfaces to suggest that our beloved image of the frontiersman is false and that what actually happened remains one of the most compelling mysteries in Texas if not the country.

In recent years, alternate versions of Davy Crockett's demise have erupted from the ashes of history, many in conflict with one another and some not nearly as glorifying as the Walt Disney version. Crockett's fate at the Alamo has become an absorbing puzzle, one that has passionate citizens of the Lone Star State divided. Strong arguments and debates have been waged over this issue in person as well as through media such as newspapers and magazines. Fistfights have been known to occasionally erupt when the topic is discussed, yet the controversy rages on.

Davy Crockett was undeniably a colorful and forceful individual. Born in Tennessee on August 17, 1786, the fifth of six children, he lived an adventurous life with few parallels in American history. Crockett served as a colonel in a local militia, scout, magistrate, justice of the peace, a member of the Tennessee legislature, and three terms as a US congressman.

Crockett, by all accounts a sensible man, became disillusioned with politics in general and President Andrew Jackson in particular. His political career came to a halt in 1836, when he was defeated in his run for reelection to Congress. Always in search of adventure, Crockett addressed his fellow congressmen on his final day in the nation's capital telling them, "You may all go to hell and I will go to Texas." And go to Texas he did, arriving in San Antonio during the first week of February 1836, with a contingent of frontiersmen he had gathered along the trail after leaving Nacogdoches, a small town in East Texas. (Some accounts maintain that Crockett handpicked a number of kindred spirits from Tennessee and Kentucky to accompany him.)

During his journey, Crockett learned of the difficulties between the Texian settlers—Anglo-American residents of Mexico Texas—and Mexico and of the siege by Mexican troops at a San Antonio mission known as the Alamo. General Santa Anna, the president-dictator of Mexico, who was often referred to as the "Napoleon of the West," was leading an army of 2,000 men, 21 cannons, 1,800 pack mules, 33 wagons, and 200 ammunition carts toward San Antonio. More soldiers and ammunition were expected to arrive during the next few days.

The Anglo settlers who lived in the region desired independence from Mexico and were prepared to achieve it by force if necessary. On learning of the impending arrival of Santa Anna's army, the residents, an estimated 183 men, volunteered to defend the town of San Antonio, taking refuge in the Alamo mission. They were accompanied by a handful of women and workers.

Crockett, according to legend, sent word to William Barret Travis, the commander of forces defending the Alamo, that he and his volunteers had come to participate in the defense of the mission and the city. After leading his men into the walled enclosure, Crockett and his contingent were assigned to the log palisade, a defensive stake fence, located between the church and the south wall.

On February 23, 1836, Santa Anna's army arrived in San Antonio and captured the town easily, no resistance having been offered. His attention was then turned to the defenders in the Alamo. His next objective was to take the mission. If his effort was met with resistance, all inside were to be killed. The general had a blood-red flag raised from an easily seen location in the town, a warning to the Alamo defenders that no quarter would be given, no prisoners taken.

On February 24, Alamo commander Travis penned a message "To the People of Texas and all Americans in the World" requesting reinforcements. On horseback, Captain Albert Martin carried the message through enemy lines to the town of Gonzales, seventy miles away. From there, couriers would take copies of it to Goliad, San Felipe, and Washington-on-the-Brazos, Nacogdoches, New Orleans, and anywhere else it was possible to deliver it. The message detailed the immediate threat by the Mexican army. Travis wrote, "I will never surrender or retreat."

On March 5, Travis learned that there would be no reinforcements. He called the defenders together and gave them the option of surrendering, attempting escape, or fighting to the death. Only one man elected to leave.

At 5 a.m. on March 6, 1836, a Sunday, Mexican general Santa Anna gave the orders for his army to charge the Alamo. It has been estimated that two thousand soldiers, cavalrymen, and artillerymen advanced upon the mission in four columns. The troopers were armed with British-made muskets, spare flints, and packs of cartridges. Many carried nine-foot-long lances, while others wielded sabers, pikes, and axes. A number of scaling ladders were carried to the mission.

The subsequent "Battle of the Alamo" was less a battle than a massacre. The Mexican columns attacked the four walls of defense at the same time. The greatest concentration of soldiers, led by

Colonel Francisco Duque, who was assisted by an aide named Enrique de la Peña, stormed the north wall defended by Travis and his assigned men. Cannons were fired against the enemy as they raced across the open field toward the mission, but once they were near the wall, the cannons became useless. Scaling ladders were propped against the wall, and as the soldiers reached the parapet, the fighting continued as close-encounter combat with swords, pistols, and close-range musket fire. Travis, who led the fighting, was struck in the head by a musket ball and fell dead.

At the foot of the Alamo's walls, the bodies of Mexican soldiers slain by the defenders began to pile up, only to be trampled over by the oncoming waves of troopers. The defenders were beginning to wither beneath the seemingly endless numbers of fighting Mexicans. To add to the already mounting difficulties, the east wall of the mission was breached, and dozens of Mexicans broke through and swarmed about the interior courtyard. At the same time, the defenders of the west wall had been overcome, and the enemy poured over the parapet and joined their comrades already inside. One of the Alamo's cannons had been captured and was turned on the defenders, killing dozens.

According to the most authoritative studies, Crockett and his remaining volunteers had retreated from the south wall and taken a position immediately in front of the church and hospital. It was at this location, claim many researchers, that the famous frontiersman met his end.

But did he? During the years since the fall of the Alamo, evidence has surfaced to suggest that this presumed demise of Davy Crockett may not have occurred at all. What truly happened to the frontier hero has generated controversy over the decades, a controversy characterized by strong opinions and intense passions, with no unanimous conclusion reached.

There have been no less than five propositions advanced relative to the fate of Davy Crockett at the Alamo. They include:

1. Crockett met his end at the top of the south wall, fighting valiantly by swinging his empty long rifle at an overwhelming force of attacking Mexican soldiers.
2. Crockett succumbed to the devastating firepower of the Mexican army, falling for a final time in front of the church.
3. Crockett was not present at the Alamo at all.
4. Crockett was taken prisoner and sentenced to spend the remainder of his life laboring in a mine deep in Mexico.
5. Crockett was captured, brought before General Santa Anna himself, and subsequently executed.

Each of these propositions deserves a response and analysis.

Noted author Dale L. Walker suggests that the "most familiar and beloved visual image of the Alamo battle is the 1903 painting by Robert Jenkins Onderdonk." In this painting, Davy Crockett is depicted holding his rifle overhead, ready to be used as a club against a horde of advancing Mexicans "through a hanging cloud of gunsmoke, through a field of dead and wounded, toward him and the half-dozen of his Tennesseans left alive." Crockett, as we have long imagined him, was wearing fringed buckskins, a hunting knife in his belt, and what may have been a coonskin cap atop his head.

For more than a century, this is the way Americans and others saw Crockett—fighting to the death for freedom. It was no accident that Walt Disney Productions employed a similar image in the popular three-part television series in 1955. In the Disney film, Crockett is atop the south wall of the Alamo, the lone defender, struggling against overwhelming odds.

Crockett may have gone down fighting to the last, but we will never know. Despite the Disney film, there exists controversy as to whether he perished on the south wall or elsewhere. In 1889, Professor George W. Noel interviewed Felix Nuñez, who had served as a sergeant on Santa Anna's army at the Alamo battle. Nuñez recalled seeing "a tall American of rather dark complexion and had on a long buckskin coat and a round cap without any bill, made out of fox skin with the long tail hanging down the back." Nuñez claimed the man had killed at least eight Mexican soldiers and wounded several others, but that the bullets from Santa Anna's army never struck him. During the fight, a "lieutenant had come over the wall . . . sprang at him, and dealt him a deadly blow with his sword, just above the right eye. . . ." Soon thereafter, according to Nuñez, the man was "pierced by not less than twenty bayonets."

The man described by Nuñez was indeed heroic, but there is no clear evidence that it was Crockett. There were more than a few men at the Alamo at the time who dressed in buckskins and wore caps of fox or coon skin.

Most researchers insist Crockett did not die at the wall but rather in the courtyard near the church. An account regarded reliable was offered by Suzanna Dickinson, the recent widow of Captain Almeron Dickinson, the Alamo's artillery commander. Ms.

Dickinson was regarded as a captive and as she was being escorted out of the Alamo grounds, she "recognized Col. Crockett lying dead and mutilated between the church and the two-story barrack building, and even remembered his peculiar cap by his side."

One of the Alamo's occupants was a slave known only as "Joe." During an interview, he stated that "Crockett and a few of the devoted friends who entered the fort with him were found lying together, with twenty-one of the enemy dead around him."

During an 1899 interview with Andrea Castañón Villanueva, she referred to "Colonel Crockett" and mentioned that she had last seen him standing in the door of the chapel and

fighting a whole column of Mexican infantry . . . Crockett stood there swinging something bright over his head. The place was full of smoke and I could not tell whether he was using a gun or a sword. A heap of dead was piled at his feet and the Mexicans were lunging at him with bayonets, but he would not retreat an inch. Crockett fell and the Mexicans poured into the Alamo.

Enrique Esparza was twelve years old and an occupant of the Alamo when it fell. He was the son of Gregorio Esparza, who died in the fight. The younger Esparza, believed to be the last of the Alamo survivors when he was interviewed in 1907, claimed that he, along with his mother, sister, and brothers, sought refuge in the church during the fight. Crockett, who Esparza called "Don Benito," was everywhere during the siege and personally slew many of the enemy with his rifle, his pistol, and his knife. He fought hand to hand. He clubbed his rifle when they closed in on him and knocked them down with its stock until he was overwhelmed by numbers and slain. . . . He immediately fell in front of the large double doors [of the church] which he defended with the force that was by his side.

The above accounts were provided by individuals who were familiar with Crockett at least to some degree. Presumably, they were able to recognize him even in death. Their testimony lends some credence to the notion that the frontiersman perished in the courtyard of the mission in front of the church. Compelling, to be sure, but there is more to examine.

Some historians have speculated that Crockett did not die at the Alamo for the simple reason, they claim, that he was never there in the first place. According to author Walker, there were newspaper accounts that stated Crockett was on a hunting trip in the Rocky Mountains.

This version is the easiest to dismiss, however. There were enough credible witnesses to establish that Crockett was, indeed, present at the Alamo during the battle. Further, if Crockett had been on a hunting trip, people would have heard of his return and aspects of his life thereafter.

A tale that was passed around within weeks following the fall of the Alamo had Crockett taken prisoner and sent to a location near Guadalajara, where he spent the remainder of his life toiling in a silver mine. One source for this bit of information was a letter penned by one William White that was printed in the *Austin City Gazette* in 1840. White claimed that on a visit to Guadalajara, he encountered an Anglo prisoner working in a mine. The man, according to White, was David Crockett. White said that Crockett wrote a letter to relatives in Tennessee and gave it to White to mail for him.

There is no evidence that the letter allegedly penned by Davy Crockett arrived at its intended destination. Despite this, John Crockett, Davy's son, heard rumors of his father's reported imprisonment in Mexico. In 1840, he undertook an investigation into the stories, but no information was ever forthcoming. The proposition that Crockett was taken prisoner and died in Mexico years after the fall of the Alamo is largely dismissed by scholars. Of all the considerations relative to how the frontiersman met his end, this one has received the least amount of attention and research.

Perhaps the most controversial theory as to the death of Davy Crockett is the notion that he survived the battle, was taken prisoner, and was subsequently executed. One year after the fall of the Alamo, Ramon Caro, Santa Anna's personal secretary, contributed a provocative item to a pamphlet that was published in Mexico. Caro stated that, following the battle proper, six survivors were discovered by General Castrillón and brought before Santa Anna. According to an article that appeared in the *New York Enquirer*:

> Six Americans were discovered near the wall yet unconquered, and who were instantly surrounded and ordered by General Castrillón to surrender. . . . David Crockett was one of the six [who] marched up boldly in front of Santa

Anna [and] looked him steadfastly in the face. Santa Anna looked at Castrillón fiercely, flew into a most violent rage, and [stated] "Have I not told you before how to dispose of them? Why do you bring them to me?" At the same time his brave officers drew and plunged their swords into the bosoms of their defenseless prisoners. . . . This was the fate of poor Crockett, and in which there can be no mistake.

Author Dan Kilgore, in his book *How Did Davy Die?*, noted that four officers and one sergeant of Santa Anna's army, all of whom participated in the battle, identified one of the captives as Davy Crockett.

In 1955, an antiques dealer in Mexico City published a diary allegedly written by a man who had witnessed the execution of Davy Crockett. The author of the diary was the aforementioned Enrique de la Peña, the aide who assisted Colonel Francisco Duque during the attack on the Alamo. Buried in its pages, wrote author Dale L. Walker, "lay a ticking bomb." One short passage mentioned that, following the fall of the Alamo, seven prisoners were brought before General Santa Anna by his aide-de-camp General Castrillón. Among them, de la Peña wrote, "was one of great stature, well proportioned, with . . . a degree of resignation and nobility that did him honor. He was the naturalist David Crockett, well known in North America for his unusual adventures. . . ." Referring to Crockett's status as a "foreigner," General Castrillón sought to intervene on his behalf but was silenced by Santa Anna "with a gesture of indignation." Santa Anna ordered an immediate execution. General Castrillón and his officers were "outraged at this action and did not support the order, hoping that once the fury of the moment had blown over, these men would be spared.

Several officers not associated with Castrillón's command, who apparently felt little sympathy toward the prisoners but keen support for General Santa Anna, "thrust themselves forward," according to de la Peña, "and with swords in hand, fell upon these unfortunate, defenseless men just as a tiger leaps upon his prey." The prisoners were tortured before they were killed. According to an article in the *New Orleans True American*, Crockett and his fellow prisoners "had cried out for quarter." Mercy.

Could this be true? Did one of America's most famous heroes beg for his life before being put to the sword? Such a proposition does not set well with the Texas and Crockett faithful.

Since 1975, according to author Walker, "virtually all writers of the Texas War of Independence in general, and of the Alamo in particular, have taken the de la Peña diary as the only reliable eyewitness account of Crockett's death." Credible Texas independence and Alamo scholars such as Mark Derr, Stephen Hardin, and others have utilized del la Peña's diary in their research and writings, subscribing to his conclusions.

Just as the de la Peña diary was securing a foothold in the interpretation of Texas history, however, along came a doubter in the form of Bill Groneman. Unimpressed with the conclusions of the academic historians, Groneman, at the time an arson investigator with the New York City Fire Department but also a deep student of the history of Texas independence, and in particular the Alamo defense, challenged the so-called experts. Groneman packed some credentials along the way. He was a member of the

Texas State Historical Association and the Alamo Society, and he has since then written several books on the Alamo and Crockett. Further, Groneman went far beyond the usual research techniques employed by the academicians. Groneman was an investigator, one who doggedly pursued the who, what, when, where, and how; a man who deconstructed the diary and analyzed every word of it and found it wanting of truth.

Groneman stated that Davy Crockett "went from a hero to a coward in the public's mind, based primarily on the translation and publication of the de la Peña diary." The publication, he claims, contains "anomalies, errors, and misinformation." He also suggests that the diary is a "complete hoax."

Off and on over a two-year span, Groneman examined de la Peña's original manuscript in the archives of the University of Texas at San Antonio. Rather than coming away convinced of what might have occurred at the Alamo, he emerged from his study with lots of questions. Among the discoveries he made were:

A. The diary "bears many indications of being a modern day fake."
B. The handwriting of more than one person was found in the diary.
C. The manuscript contained numerous errors, as well as the use of phrases that only came into use decades later.
D. The diary was dated 1936, but it contained information from sources that did not exist prior to that year.
E. The provenance of the diary was never established. Sanchez Garza, the owner and original publisher never provided any

information relative to how he came into possession of the document.

F. There existed odd similarities between the de la Peña diary and *The Journal of Jean Lafitte*, a 1958 vanity publication and a clear forgery by a man named John Andrechyne Laflin. Renowned national handwriting expert Charles Hamilton exposed Laflin in his book *Great Forgers and Famous Fakes*. Groneman also connected Laflin to Alamo studies—Laflin was believed to have been the forger of a letter written by an Alamo defender. As a result, Groneman and Hamilton tend to believe that he "wrote" the de la Peña diary.

Today, numerous Alamo and Crockett scholars and writers as well as enthusiasts remain in disagreement over whether or not the de la Peña diary is authentic or a fake.

Bill Groneman concludes his studies by stating that, in the end, there is not enough evidence for determining exactly how Davy Crockett died. Passionate responses from various viewpoints have erupted and controversy continues to rage, yet the mystery remains unsolved.

SELECTED REFERENCES/ SUGGESTED READINGS

Babcock, Bernie. *Booth and the Spirit of Lincoln*. New York: Grossett & Dunlap, 1925.

Balsiger, David, and Charles E. Sellier. *The Lincoln Conspiracy*. Los Angeles: Schick-Sunn Classic Books, 1977.

Bates, Finis L. *The Escape and Suicide of John Wilkes Booth, Assassin of President Lincoln*. Memphis: Pilcher Printing, 1907.

Croy, Homer. *Jesse James Was My Neighbor*. New York: Duell, Sloan, & Pierce, 1949.

Davis, William C. *The Pirate Laffite: The Treacherous World of the Corsairs of the Gulf*. New York: Houghton Mifflin Harcourt, 2006.

de la Peña, José Enrique. *With Santa Anna in Texas: Narrative of the Revolution*. Translated and edited by Carmen Perry. College Station: Texas A&M University Press, 1975.

Derr, Mark. *The Frontiersman: The Real Life and Many Legends of Davy Crockett*. New York: William Morrow, 1993.

Fell, Barry. *America B.C.: Ancient Settlers in the New World*. New York: Pocket (rev. ed.), 1989.

Hardin, Stephen L. *Texian Iliad: A Military History of the Texas Revolution*. Austin: University of Texas Press, 1994.

Garrett, Patrick F. *The Authentic Life of Billy, the Kid*. Santa Fe: New Mexican Print. and Pub. Co., 1882.

Groneman, Bill. *Eyewitness to the Alamo*. Guilford, CT: Lone Star Books, 2017.

———. *Death of a Legend: The Myth and Mystery Surrounding the Death of Davy Crockett*. Guilford, CT: Taylor Trade Publishing, 1999.

———. *Defense of a Legend: Crockett and the de la Peña Diary*. Plano, TX: Republic of Texas Press, 1994.

Hall, Frank, and Whitten, Lindsey. *Jesse James Rides Again*. Lawton, OK: LaHoma Publishing Company, 1948.

Jameson, W. C. *Billy the Kid: Investigating History's Mysteries*. Guilford, CT: Twodot, 2018.

———. *Texas Train Robberies*. Guilford, CT: Lone Star Books, 2017.

———. *John Wilkes Booth: Beyond the Grave*. Lanham, MD: Taylor Trade Publishing, 2013.

———. *Lost Treasures in American History*. Boulder, CO: Taylor Trade Publishing, 2006.

———. *Billy the Kid: Beyond the Grave*. Boulder, CO: Taylor Trade Publishing, 2005.

———. *Buried Treasures of Texas*. Little Rock, AR: August House Publishers, Inc., 1991.

———. *Buried Treasures of the American Southwest*. Little Rock, AR: August House Publishers, Inc., 1989.

Kaldec, Robert F. *They "Knew" Billy the Kid: Interviews with Old-Time New Mexicans*. Santa Fe, NM: Ancient City Press, 1987.

Kilgore, Dan, *How Did Davy Die and Why Do We Care So Much?* College Station: Texas A & M University Press, 2010.

Metz, Leon. *Pat Garrett: The Story of a Western Lawman*. Norman: University of Oklahoma Press, 1974.

Miles, Elton. *Stray Tales of the Big Bend*. College Station: Texas A & M University Press, 1993.

———. *More Tales of the Big Bend*. College Station: Texas A & M University Press, 1988.

———. *Tales of the Big Bend*. College Station: Texas A & M University Press, 1976.

Nolan, F. *The Lincoln County War: A Documentary History*. Norman: University of Oklahoma Press, 1992.

Radford, Benjamin. *Mysterious New Mexico: Miracles, Magic, and Monsters in the Land of Enchantment*. Albuquerque: University of New Mexico Press, 2014.

Ramsay, Jack C. *Jean Laffite: Prince of Pirates*. Woodway, TX: Eakin Press, 1996.

Sonnichsen, C. L., and Morrison, William V. *Alias Billy the Kid.* Albuquerque: University of New Mexico Press, 1955.

Stern, Phillip Van Doren. *The Man Who Killed Lincoln.* New York: The World Publishing Company, 1942.

Turilli, Rudy. *I Knew Jesse James.* Self-published. 1966.

Walker, Dale L. *Legends and Lies: Great Mysteries of the American West.* New York: A Tom Doherty Associates Book, 1997.

Wood, Joe. *My Jesse James Story.* Washington, MO: The Washington Missourian, 1989.

ACKNOWLEDGMENTS

A huge debt of gratitude is extended to the late, great, award-winning Texas author, friend, and mentor Dale L. Walker. Walker was always attracted to a good mystery and systematically went about deconstructing them, subjecting each and every part to deep and intense analysis, and ultimately arriving at a solution. His efforts have been manifested in a couple of books devoted to the topic of unsolved mysteries: *Legends and Lies* and *The Calamity Papers*. I have lost count of the hours Dale and I discussed these and other mysteries, why they appeal to us, and why we can't turn loose of them.

Author Bill Groneman has long been interested in the Texas revolution and the Battle of the Alamo, and his research has yielded some fascinating books on these topics. Groneman is an inspirational explorer into the world of mystery as it relates to historical events and figures in Texas. There is an old saying that goes "History repeats itself, and historians repeat one another." We have found this to be true in our own studies. Groneman, not content with merely looking something up and repeating it, puts on his investigator's hat and delves deeply into whatever mystery or conundrum sparks his interest, searching for provenance, answers, results. The academic historians can learn a lot from him.

It is a pleasure to be associated with the Rowman & Littlefield publishing family and all of its imprints that I have been connected with. Many authors I know view the writing and editing process a chore, a task. I have never felt that way. The R & L folks, always professional and experienced in my dealings with them, have made it fun and keep me looking forward to the next project.

I have been associated with literary agent Sandra Bond for well over a decade. She is to be admired for her patience in putting up with my ignorance of all things technical and somehow manages to place nearly every manuscript I send her.

Laurie Jameson—accomplished memoirist, novelist, poet, and editor—is my first reader and editor on all book projects. It is due to her efforts that my manuscripts arrive at the publishing company's desk considerably cleaner than they were when I handed them to her.

INDEX

ABOUT THE AUTHOR

W. C. Jameson is the award-winning author of over 100 books and more than 1,500 articles. Several of his writings have been adapted for television, documentaries, and film, and he has served as an advisor, narrator, and expert on a variety of subjects for the History Channel, the Travel Channel, the American Heroes Channel, the Westerns Channel, PBS, NPR, and more. In 2019, he was inducted into the Colorado Writers Hall of Fame. He lives and writes in Texas.